Challenging
Perfectionism

of related interest

Teen Anxiety
A CBT and ACT Activity Resource Book for Helping Anxious Adolescents
Raychelle Cassada Lohmann
ISBN 978 1 84905 969 5
eISBN 978 0 85700 859 6

Appearance Anxiety
A Guide to Understanding Body Dysmorphic Disorder
for Young People, Families and Professionals
National and Specialist OCD, BDD and Related
Disorders Service, Maudsley Hospital
ISBN 978 1 78592 456 9
eISBN 978 1 78450 832 6

The Mental Health and Wellbeing Handbook for Schools
Transforming Mental Health Support on a Budget
Clare Erasmus
Foreword by Chris Edwards
ISBN 978 1 78592 481 1
eISBN 978 1 78450 869 2

Challenging Perfectionism

An Integrative Approach for Supporting Young People Using ACT, CBT and DBT

Dawn Starley

Jessica Kingsley Publishers
London and Philadelphia

First published in Great Britain in 2021 by Jessica Kingsley Publishers

An Hachette Company

1

Copyright © Dawn Starley 2021

Appendix D is reproduced with kind permission of Oxford High School.

Front cover image source: Shutterstock®.

Trigger Warning: This book mentions suicide.

A CIP catalogue record for this title is available from the British Library and the Library of Congress

ISBN 978 1 78775 393 8
eISBN 978 1 78775 394 5

Printed and bound in the United States by Offset Paperback Manufacturers Inc

Jessica Kingsley Publishers' policy is to use papers that are natural, renewable and recyclable products and made from wood grown in sustainable forests. The logging and manufacturing processes are expected to conform to the environmental regulations of the country of origin.

Jessica Kingsley Publishers
73 Collier Street
London N1 9BE, UK

www.jkp.com

To Sophie, my 'perfect match'.

For Margot and Teddy, I'm so proud to be your mummy.

And Hugo, thank you for choosing me.

Finally, for anyone who has ever had a 'perfectionist' thought that made them feel they were not 'good enough'. You are. Just the way you are.

Contents

Disclaimers

This book was produced following a thorough review of the current literature – both academic and in popular culture – on perfectionism in students, and in discussion with a range of professionals, including educational psychologists, a child and adolescent psychiatrist, an art psychotherapist, a cognitive-behavioural therapist, a dialectical behaviour therapist, an integrative counsellor and a lead specialist practitioner in psychotherapy for personality disorders. It is based upon my doctoral thesis 'Exploring and challenging perfectionism in four high-achieving UK secondary schools' and the related article 'Perfectionism: A challenging but worthwhile research area for educational psychology' (Starley 2018). All attempts have been made to reference the sources of my information where possible.

It must be noted that the literature on supporting students high in perfectionism is very sparse; this book represents an early attempt to bring together what is known worldwide to have practical application for schools and families. It uses frameworks incorporating cognitive-behavioural and psychodynamic principles. There is a strong focus on systemic support for the student, along with developing individual competencies, predominantly coping skills (including the acceptance of life's challenges).

The premise for this book was based on my experiences as a student at an independent girls' grammar school, working in young adult mental health support and in classroom teaching, the culmination of which was the realisation that 'perfectionist' students are a group potentially at risk of later mental health problems, and are likely to be currently under-supported in schools. This book seeks to raise awareness of these students and consider ways in which their needs can best be supported at home and in school.

The idea of 'optimalism' is entirely that of Tal Ben-Shahar in his 2009 book *The Pursuit of Perfect*. Interested readers are recommended this book; full details can be found in the References section.

Preface

A daunting task indeed, to write a book on perfectionism. Will people be expecting perfection, or something close to it?

To have had the 'perfect' conditions for writing this book would have been wonderful: unlimited time; free from distractions, interruptions, unexpected events, a busy job and complicated family life; a comfortable workspace with reliable technology; good health and ideas that kept flowing on demand.

But that is not life.

It is not the real world.

The real world is messy, and unpredictable, with compromises where you envisioned solutions in your favour. This book was written in snatched moments between child and pet care, including unexpected hospital and vet trips. Writing this also revolved around work responsibilities, partner illness and babies learning to roll, crawl and walk...whole new levels of mobility requiring massively enhanced supervision. Late nights, prioritising and organisation skills beyond anything I'd ever experienced, and the unending support of my nearest and dearest who are no doubt sick of anything that remotely comes close to sounding like perfectionism, were the order of business for what you are now reading.

Not 'perfect', perhaps, but complete. Achieved. Done!

And that, right there, is the premise for this book. The 'messiness' of life, and our ability – or lack of ability – to control it. To control what happens to us, for us, and perhaps most importantly, *within* us. It is not about waiting for 'the perfect moment', but rather taking what you have available and making the best of it. Using your time wisely and with purpose. For it is only when we put aside our quest for 'perfect' that we can embrace true creativity. And with creativity comes freedom and the authentic enjoyment of all life has to offer, beyond basic survival.

A professional interest...

Perfectionism has resonated throughout my career. It made an appearance in service-users during my time as a mental health support worker, in pupils with Special Educational Needs during my time as a learning support assistant and pupils without any apparent additional needs during my time as a teacher. In my current occupation as an educational psychologist rarely a day goes past when I don't identify aspects of perfectionism in school staff, young people or parents, or indeed in the cultural influences all around us. My role has brought into sharp focus the urgent need for a clear response to 'perfectionist' attitudes in students and schools as I am sadly witnessing higher expectations on staff and young people, increased rates of mental health problems amongst children and a desire amongst families and school staff to change things for the better with the frustration of not knowing how to do so within limited resources. Although many schools claim to promote a 'growth mindset' culture in policy and sometimes in practice, I wonder how effective this is for something perhaps as engrained as perfectionism and within such a fiercely pressurised culture of attainment. Something more...something different is needed.

This is where this book comes in; the culmination of doctoral research into perfectionism in young people to provide the timely combination of theory and practical guidance from those 'in the know'. Combined with the expertise of a range of education and health professionals (see Appendix A for more information), I have contributed my own knowledge gained from studying Educational, Child and Community Psychology, Applied Forensic Psychology, Mindfulness, Mindset Performance, Acceptance and Commitment Therapy, Cognitive-Behavioural Therapy, Dialectical Behaviour Therapy, Drawing and Talking Therapy, Therapeutic

Art, Counselling, Crisis Support, Supervision, Mental Health and Psychiatry. The strategies in this book have been carefully compiled using a comprehensive grounding of theory, supported by research, and shaped by the invaluable contributions of professionals working daily with young people affected by perfectionism. As a result, they offer a hopeful approach to challenging perfectionism and one on which future research may build.

On a personal note...

I am proud to say I am passionate about perfectionism, having come to the conclusion that I am a 'recovering perfectionist'. This was a humorous yet poignant phrase used by one of the adult participants in my doctoral research study, during our discussion of perfectionism which talked about the concept in terms not dissimilar from the world of addiction and recovery. It is also a phrase used by Ben-Shahar in his book, *The Pursuit of Perfect* (2009), which dramatically helped to shape my own approach to life along with the concepts in what you are now reading.

As a parent I have learned the true necessity of discarding perfectionist beliefs and replacing them with much healthier and functional attitudes that help keep me sane amongst the situational insanity of raising two young children (one of whom has a life-shortening genetic condition with complex medical needs), supporting a partner launching a new, life-changing business, and trying to provide a competent service as Educational Psychologist to the Local Authority. Not to mention the other 'responsibilities' of life: being a good friend, a contributing member of the extended family, promoting positive social change where possible and trying to maintain a healthy diet, exercise and sleep regime. Life is a complex and delicate balancing act; try to juggle too much without the skills or environment to do so and something will inevitably get 'dropped'.

I still notice the occasional unhelpful thought or catch myself perseverating or procrastinating. I sometimes find myself tense and realise I am pushing away emotions rather than allowing myself to really feel them. But recognising these things is huge progress, and I have strategies to challenge them. I know these strategies are working because, on the whole, I have a much healthier attitude towards myself and life than I once did. I cope daily with a complex balance of work and life commitments. I am efficient with my use of time, prioritise according to my values and therefore enjoy both a fulfilling professional *and* personal life. The strategies I use mean that every day I am moving further from perfectionism and towards a healthier way of being. Success *and* happiness. It is possible. I am a wholehearted believer in the power of the strategies shared in this book and I am hopeful they may also be of value to you and your young people.

A note of thanks...

This book would not have come to be without the contributions of everyone involved in my doctoral research, not least of all my research supervisors, Dr Andrew Richards and Dr Martin Levinson, who believed in my passion to change the world for the better and helped me take a 'ballet shoe' rather than 'welly boot' approach to doing so. Many thanks also to Dr Shirley Larkin, Margaret Tunbridge and everyone at Jessica Kingsley Publishers who helped to shape my research to be suitable for publication. I'd like to extend my thanks to all the students, teachers and parents, including my own, who helped me truly understand the scope and depths of perfectionism, and to the professionals who helped me 'see the light' about strategies to help challenge perfectionism. You are all part of this book.

There are two writers I cannot fail to mention in the development of this book, people who have taken on 'guru'-like status in my world: Tal Ben-Shahar for introducing me to the idea of 'optimalism' from which I have never looked back, and Brené Brown for talking with courage and authenticity about shame and vulnerability, and how to 'dare greatly' in our classrooms. I have not (yet) had the privilege of meeting either of you in person, but you have taught me so much; thank you.

Finally, a note of thanks to my critical social support network who over the years have showed me that, despite presenting as being 'very together', I don't have to do it alone, and have enriched my life as a result. My supportive family and extended family, in particular Dad, Sophie and Pussa, and of course the memory of my Mum. To my loyal friends Sadie, Siobhan and Jennie who have always accepted me exactly as I am, my wise supervisors of integrity Sam, Margie and Jenny who, post-training, have become friends with whom I can share joys as well as challenges, and finally to my brilliant therapists, Diane and Kat; you have all changed my world for the better. Perhaps my most precious thanks goes to a very special lady; Countess Shelagh Noel De Fane Edge Morgan Skarbek. It was in your home, in which I was made to feel so welcome, with your 'brain food' and talks of psychoanalysis, politics and philosophy, that the ideas in this book sprang to life in my mind. Thank you.

For you, the reader...

No matter what our age, experience, qualifications or wisdom, there is still always something to be learned. I hope you enjoy the journey and take something from what you read for the young people in your life. I also hope you feel confident that when I talk about strategies to challenge perfectionism, I am not only talking about what I know as a psychologist, from the research, practice and scientific theory, but I am also sharing with you the things that have worked for me.

Introduction

The complex world of perfectionism

Perfectionism is a challenging topic to work with.

First, there is no universal definition of perfectionism, and in fact a vast array of terminology to describe what may or may not be similar concepts exists, e.g.:

- 'normal' and 'neurotic' perfectionism[1]

- 'positive' and 'negative' perfectionism[2]

- 'adaptive', 'maladaptive', and 'non'-perfectionism[3]

- and just simply 'perfectionism'.[4]

For the purposes of this book I have focused on what some researchers might describe as 'maladaptive', 'neurotic' or 'negative' perfectionism. I prefer to think of it as simply 'perfectionism', as I am in agreement with American perfectionism researcher Greenspon:[5] to consider there may be any positive or healthy associations with perfectionism is unhelpful and might actually be part of a damaging cycle. More on this later.

My definition also relates to 'socially-prescribed' perfectionism; that is, 'the perception that others demand perfection from the self'[6] or 'evaluative concerns' perfectionism, described as vulnerability to negative psychological outcomes due to 'motives and values predominantly derived from pressures in the social environment'.[7] Not only do these have strong links in the research with negative outcomes, they also offer the potential for systemic intervention when considering the 'others' and 'social environment' that are being perceived to be exerting the pressure for perfection.

A second difficulty in working with perfectionism includes being able to actually research the individuals of interest; those students who take part in research studies are likely to be high in motivation to change or at least understand themselves better, and therefore unrepresentative of those students who are reluctant to ask for help for fear of being exposed,[8] or of those lacking self-awareness of their difficulties. Additionally, most research studies use self-rating scales to measure perfectionism; there is no guarantee that these are answered honestly or with self-reflection, and since different rating scales are used in different studies, participants can't easily be compared. Sample sizes for research are often small, so generalising is a challenge. They also tend to be limited to the Higher Education population and usually those considered 'gifted'. This clearly misses a significant 'chunk' of the student population who are not only younger but who may *not* be considered to be of high ability. Finally, the majority of perfectionism research has been with the adult clinical population which perhaps emphasises the importance of early intervention and a need to better understand perfectionism in young people.

Despite these difficulties, perfectionism remains an important area for research and one of growing interest, as there are increasing claims of links with a range of negative outcomes, yet there are also conflicting beliefs that perfectionism may be a good thing. These will be discussed briefly next, and in more detail in Chapters 2 and 3.

Risks and perceived benefits

There is a strong theme running through the existing perfectionism research about problematic outcomes of perfectionism, particularly relating to the development and prolongation of a range of mental health problems in young people and adults.[9] The following notable links have been made with high levels of perfectionism:

- anxiety[10]

- depression[11]

- obsessive-compulsive disorder[12]

- eating disorders[13]

- autism spectrum condition,[14] including Asperger's Syndrome[15]

- attention deficit hyperactivity disorder.[16]

A particularly concerning link has been made between perfectionism and suicide. Suicide is among the leading causes of death in young people[17] and can have a devastating impact on families and communities. The major premise for this book is the under-recognised link that is increasingly being made between high levels of perfectionism and suicide;[18] recent suggestions are that it may be a bigger risk factor than previously thought.[19]

Suicide rates amongst young people (aged between 15 and 24) in America, Australia and the UK are at the highest they have been in over a decade, with New Zealand having been found to have the highest rate of teen suicide in the developed world.[20] A UK report revealed that almost a third of young people have contemplated or attempted suicide,[21] citing contributing factors which may be related to perfectionism: pressure from schoolwork, feeling like a failure, fear of the future, lack of confidence and a sense of isolation.[22] This may be particularly pertinent among young men (for whom suicide is the leading cause of death), as suicidal intentions and vulnerability may be difficult to detect when hidden behind a perfectionistic need to preserve an image of flawless competency.[23] Secrecy about mental health problems and suicidality, a recognised feature of adolescence,[24] is likely to be heightened for those high in self-stigma (the belief that they are not capable), whose accomplishments may deflect attention from feelings of inadequacy and self-destructive tendencies.[25] Further, students who are cooperative and compliant in school,[26] as is perhaps the case for those high in perfectionism, may be overlooked due to perceived competency and act impulsively upon their hidden psychological distress.[27]

Flett and Hewitt, leading researchers in perfectionism, describe the link between perfectionistic self-criticism, self-doubt and suicide as an important public health issue to be addressed,[28] but there is little knowledge of the awareness of this or how to address it amongst school staff, parents, or young people themselves. This book begins to fill this gap.

Confusingly, there is a competing viewpoint that perfectionism is a positive thing. Some researchers link perfectionism with achievement, and this has clear implications when considering the above risks. If people think perfectionism is what helps someone achieve success then it is likely to be reinforced, perhaps despite the associated risks. This book takes the view, in agreement with several notable researchers in the area, that there is no such thing as 'positive perfectionism' and that any related 'benefits' are likely to be short-lived and serve a less than healthy function for the individual. This is discussed more in Chapter 3.

The need for this book

When researching my doctoral thesis I could find no clear guide to perfectionism written from a systemic perspective, nor anything specifically addressing a UK context, yet in my role as an educational psychologist I frequently experienced parents and teachers asking for, and appreciating, any guidance on how to address what appeared to be problematic perfectionism in their students. The lack of research into awareness, understanding and interventions in schools is a significant concern, since this is a potentially vulnerable group who:

- are unlikely to meet thresholds for working with other professional services if they are predominantly well behaved and high-achieving while at school,

- are unlikely to be considered 'perfectionists' if they are not those things, so their underlying difficulty may be missed or misunderstood.

Schools are the primary source of mental health treatment for young people[29] and appear to be natural places for interventions,[30] since teachers spend a large amount of time with young people and have access to specialist resources, so are in a good position to provide support throughout the school day. School has an important environmental role to play in portraying healthy beliefs about achievement and striving, and proactively challenging unhelpful cognitions regarding acceptance and self-worth which may lead to performance-hindering anxiety. Since a major risk factor for students high in perfectionism is their reluctance to seek help when needed, Flett and Hewitt (2014) argued that schools need a proactive approach to ensure they are meeting the needs of vulnerable students, for example conveying the message that seeking help is not a weakness, and being extremely alert to students who appear to be doing exceptionally well in ways that seem incongruous with prevailing stressors and challenges. However, these authors suggested an 'ideal prevention program' in which schools help students to *lower* their standards, which is likely to meet resistance in our current, 'outcomes-driven' educational climate. Their suggestion of engaging parents in interventions, however, is highly aligned with current educational thinking. This book is also addressed to parents who play a vital role in helping to shape their children's emotional wellbeing and promoting successful outcomes.

My ecosystemic approach is congruent with Greenspon's notion that perfectionism is intersubjective and 'arises out of the interaction between the worlds of experience of two or more people',[31] rather than the motivation coming from entirely within the student. A societal issue exists, at least in the UK, that more than half of adults lack the confidence to approach a child if they suspect they have a mental health problem in case they are mistaken;[32] this may also apply to parents and teachers, particularly where no specific training has been provided. There is little evidence of the inclusion of perfectionism in initial teacher training courses and therefore an assumption that perhaps there is no perceived need, or that it takes lower priority than other 'issues' for trainee teachers. I am aware of no teacher or parent training courses currently being offered that address perfectionism specifically and, as previously mentioned, no clear guidance for school staff and parents. Thinking psychodynamically, it is likely that teachers' own levels and experiences of perfectionism will affect their attitudes towards students high in perfectionism, however research in this area relates only to teacher perfectionism, and professional achievement[33] and burnout,[34] rather than how it affects their teaching practice on a relational level.

The level of understanding and awareness of parents about perfectionism is also unknown; their attitudes are also likely to be influenced by their own levels and experiences of perfectionism. What is more readily available is information about the knowledge and understanding of parents regarding emotional wellbeing more generally, which highlights a high level of concern. For example, research by Action for Children suggests that UK parents, particularly mothers, are more likely to worry about their children's emotional wellbeing than any other health issues[35] and a recent survey by Young Minds found that two-thirds of parents felt there was a lack of resources available to support young people with mental health problems.[36] However a Place2Be survey found almost a third of parents of children aged 5–18 admitted they would feel embarrassed if their child wanted counselling in school, and one in five would not encourage their child to take this up, even if they asked for it.[37] This supports the need for a more systemic approach to addressing perfectionism that does not stigmatise the young person or their family.

This book is therefore relevant for young people, families and schools in the current educational and political climate. Although this book aims to be applicable worldwide, the foremost premise is for it to have value amongst the schools and families I work with, here in the UK, as there is no other resource available to support schools with this specific topic. However, there is no reason why the explanations, understanding and strategies cannot also be applied elsewhere in the world; regardless of culture, the ideas remain generalisable across students. I welcome feedback from readers abroad, or indeed in the UK, who may wish to suggest edits for future editions of this work.

Lack of early or systemic intervention

Evidence suggests that perfectionism increases over time[38] and is 'notoriously difficult to treat' in adults.[39] Various American resources for schools, parents and children advocate early intervention[40] but there has been little systematic work exploring this. If, as suggested by the predominance of Higher Education studies in the existing research literature, perfectionists are perhaps more likely to be high-achievers, who are unlikely to seek support when required and who perhaps develop mental health problems only once they have left school, it is possible that schools fail to support such 'at-risk' students, since they may present no real problems within school. However, through my work as an educational psychologist in the UK, I am aware of many students who display problematic behaviours resembling perfectionism nearing public examination time, with school staff feeling helpless to provide meaningful support, resulting in frustration for all concerned and ultimately *underachievement*. It may therefore be that underachievers are high in perfectionism!

The research literature suggests little in the way of systemic intervention, yet adults have the skills and power to effect change more easily than perhaps young people do for themselves. This is particularly the case where strong defence mechanisms, including lack of self-awareness, exist, as is likely with perfectionism. This lack of early or systemic intervention is of great concern, as there is much that could be done with very little training or resources! I hope that this book provides an accessible account of strategies that can be used by any adult working with young people. There are also sections for the young people themselves, and I hope that these are easy to understand and follow so that early intervention can be effective.

Using approaches from popular psychotherapeutic interventions, this book aims to support young people's mental health in three ways:

1. reduce high levels of perfectionism

2. challenge views which may be serving to promote or reinforce perfectionism

3. increase levels of a 'positive opposite' of perfectionism.

The strategies outlined in this book 'make sense' when perfectionism is understood to the depth addressed over the following chapters. However, it must be noted that there has not yet been any substantial research done to support their integrated use with young people high in perfectionism. We are in desperate need of quality research into 'what works' for young people high in perfectionism, as highlighted in the first part of my doctoral research published in the journal *Educational Psychology in Practice*.[41] The second part of my doctoral research (unpublished...yet) indicated a highly positive response to this approach from students high in perfectionism, their school staff and parents, across four schools and 32 participants in the UK, as well as nine professionals from a variety of health and education backgrounds. This integrative approach, as outlined here, offers hope for challenging perfectionism and improving outcomes for vulnerable young people. It comes with the caveat that it is in its infancy in terms of validation in the research world. I would welcome any researchers to pursue this piece of work.

The current climate

Schools are under increased pressure to achieve high academic standards for all students.[42] In the UK this is a combination of pressure felt systemically due to Ofsted's 'satisfactory' category being replaced with the more demanding label: 'requires improvement', which carries consequences for the future of the school, including possible dismissal of Senior Leadership, and pressure on staff due to the increase in academies and performance-related pay.

Teaching unions in the UK have suggested that changes within the education system have placed 'unnecessary stress' on the school community.[43] When considering the psychodynamic impact of teaching and learning, it is also relevant that recent news reports suggest 'teacher stress levels in England are soaring'.[44] This applies to both organisational psychodynamics, for example as explored by Obholzer and Roberts (1994) within 'human services', and those at an individual level, for example as discussed by Salzberger-Wittenberg, Williams and Osborne (1999). The effect of these additional stress factors upon students high in perfectionism is unexplored; however, my understanding of psychodynamic theory applied to both individuals and groups suggests a potential area of concern: such pressured environments could put those high in perfectionism at risk of mental ill health. Due to an already elevated sense of pressure on themselves, there is only so much pressure an individual can withstand and perhaps pressure coming from within as well as without would be too much for some to tolerate.

There is particular interest in the existing research around perfectionism in the high-achieving population, with debates over achievement encouraging[45] or acting as a safeguard against[46] 'maladaptive perfectionism'. If students high in perfectionism are likely to also be high-achievers, schools may fail to notice or ignore signs of internalised distress in these students as they present high value to the school as 'star pupils';[47] other students may present with greater 'need' of emotional support and staff may even fear that attainment will *decrease* if resources are spent addressing high-achievers' emotional wellbeing.

Student emotional wellbeing is a current school priority, demonstrated through Ofsted's greater focus on Safeguarding, and the popularity of interventions such as Thrive, Nurture Groups, mindfulness and ELSAs (Emotional Literacy Support Assistants). A major challenge perceived by schools is balancing the improvement of attainment with improving emotional wellbeing, without one jeopardising the other. In their 'Nurture Group' materials for staff, Bennathan and Boxall stated in reference to younger children that 'emotional and cognitive development cannot...be considered separately'.[48] Older students' cognitive development may also benefit from their emotional wellbeing being supported, reflecting Maslow's (1970) Hierarchy of Human Needs model, which remains popular in contemporary educational psychology and is explored more later.

The situation regarding emotional wellbeing is largely mirrored across the globe; for example, in Canada a recent news report stated that 'focus on achievement is destroying education',[49] recognising the pressures on school leaders to boost attainment data within limited budgets yet highlighting that this leads to a 'culture of neglect'. An American news report described a 'hidden mental health crisis in American schools',[50] indicating particularly high rates of anxiety in students and reduced resources for schools to meet these emotional wellbeing needs. Meradji (2018) explained that mental health has become 'an urgent matter' and described the introduction of a 'mental health curriculum' across Californian schools to begin to address this need, urging all American schools to implement such an approach. In Australia, it is recognised that 'mental health education remains a token gesture of the Australian curriculum',[51] with clinical psychologist Manning (2017) highlighting the need for Australian students to learn the practical skills needed for good mental health, not just the theory. Emotional wellbeing is clearly an increasingly high priority internationally, with debates ongoing about how best to support this with limited resources.

Relating to education and emotional wellbeing, high levels of perfectionism have been linked with:

- school refusal[52]

- insomnia[53]

- headaches[54]

- the socially problematic expression of anger,[55] including both physical and verbal aggression.[56]

As already mentioned, and providing a conflicting view, high levels of perfectionism have also been linked with achievement, engagement, emotional wellbeing and positive outcomes.[57] This disparity is a relevant issue for those of us who have influential roles in the lives of young people; how we as 'key adults' choose to respond is likely to depend on our own beliefs about the risks and benefits of perfectionism. And how we respond is likely to either challenge or reinforce perfectionism in our young people. We have a lot of power!

Flett and Hewitt assert that perfectionism is 'highly prevalent among children and adolescents',[58] supporting the suggestion that, internationally, over a quarter of students are 'maladaptive perfectionists'.[59] The scale of the issue is not entirely clear due to confusion in the literature relating to different definitions of perfectionism and categories of perfectionist, discrepancies over its origin and whether or not it is beneficial or harmful, and conflict over how to measure and 'treat' it. However, perfectionism may affect more students than previously thought and hence underlie many issues causing concern for schools, particularly considering its link with autism spectrum condition, attention deficit hyperactivity disorder, anxiety and school refusal. It therefore follows that raising awareness amongst school staff and parents over the risks of perfectionism and associated individual needs is key to promoting positive change.

More and younger children are being prescribed antidepressants and waiting lists to access child and adolescent mental health services can often be months long. Schools' focus on children's mental health reflects the current political agenda, with arguments from senior NHS England and Department of Health officials that it should become a national ambition with increased funding and school input,[60] recognising that it has been chronically underfunded for decades.[61] This acknowledges the increased rates of stress and related mental health problems amongst UK school students;[62] for example, two large teaching associations claimed that schools are struggling to deal with rising numbers of students self-harming, due to reduced access to specialist support,[63] and there has been particular interest over recent years in the potentially harmful effects of social media on young people's mental health, as highlighted in this excerpt from *The Guardian*:

> social media is harming the mental health of teenagers...the pressure to be perfect and always 'on' is overwhelming.[64]

Students high in perfectionism could be amongst the most vulnerable of these due to self-induced pressures and self-defeating attributions of their experiences, and their link with eating disorders and self-harm.[65]

Large amounts of funding have been recently provided to children's services and the NHS for addressing mental health needs as early as possible, reflecting the argument that early care is better for individuals in the long term and is also value for money.[66] Tackling the 'root causes' of problems helps to ensure public services remain sustainable in the long term.[67] This is significant, since around half of young adults with mental health problems experience difficulties before they are 15.[68] There is direct relevance for schools in developing earlier, school-based intervention and formal tuition on mental health, particularly considering the increasing pressures facing our Child and Adolescent Mental Health Services (CAMHS).[69] Many students who could benefit from psychological support may not meet the increasingly high thresholds needed to access services, or their likelihood for self-presentation and self-concealment[70] means they are unlikely to seek help when needed.[71] When this denial of needing help and/or reluctance to seek help is combined with the alarming fact that those high in perfectionism are more likely than others to complete any attempted suicides due to their 'thorough and precise suicide plans',[72] students high in perfectionism may be extremely vulnerable due to this double risk. The introduction of the Social, Emotional and Mental Health category of Special Educational Needs and Disability[73] further recognises this political priority and helps to ensure schools are more aware of 'invisible' conditions. This goes some way towards removing perceived embarrassment and increasing the likelihood that signs are spotted and acted upon.[74]

A focus on students' mental health and emotional wellbeing has also been brought to the awareness of parents, through media reports of increased rates of stress and related mental health problems amongst schoolchildren.[75] This includes increases in self-harming, anxiety and depression,[76] conditions highly correlated with perfectionism,[77] along with cases of high-achieving student suicides.[78]

Taking all this into account, my aims for this book are for you to have:

- a greater knowledge and understanding of perfectionism in young people

- an increased awareness of the risks associated with perfectionism

- a range of helpful strategies you can use to support students high in perfectionism move towards healthier ways of living.

This book is arranged into eight chapters:

- Chapter 1 introduces you to the concept of perfectionism.

- Chapter 2 highlights the risks associated with high levels of perfectionism.

- Chapter 3 explains the illusory benefits of perfectionism.

- Chapter 4 explores a 'positive opposite' of perfectionism.

- Chapter 5 considers the bigger picture in terms of cultural perfectionism and the influence of this on schools and families.

- Chapter 6 offers you practical guidance in planning for supporting students high in perfectionism, including considering the principles of and targets for support.

- Chapter 7 provides practical 'ABC' strategies for you – the adults in the young person's life – to challenge perfectionism and support students towards a healthier, 'optimalist' attitude. There is also a whole-school approach and a 'quick guide' to considerations when supporting young people high in perfectionism.

- Chapter 8 is dedicated entirely to the young person who is ready and willing to try something new. The same ABC strategies are here, along with ideas about how young people can apply these to themselves.

- There is also a range of resources for you in the Appendices, and a full list of references and further reading ideas for those interested.

To conclude, I am always happy to hear from those interested in the topic, whether you agree with my ideas or not. In fact, if you disagree, all the better. Being able to face challenge with an open mind and allowing yourself to be vulnerable enough to take the risk that you might be wrong, might not know all the answers, and might even be disliked because of your views, is a marker that perfectionism is slipping away and being replaced with a healthier attitude to the world. Let's communicate openly and help to move things forward in this fascinating area of psychology, education and life.

I can be contacted directly through my professional pages on LinkedIn or Facebook, or via email at *Dawnstarley@icloud.com*.

Endnotes

1 Hamachek (1978)
2 Chan (2007)
3 Gnilka, Ashby and Noble (2012)
4 Beevers and Miller (2004)
5 Greenspon (2000)
6 Flett, Hewitt and Cheng (2008, p.196)
7 Mallinson *et al.* (2014, p.975)
8 Onwuegbuzie and Daley (1999)
9 Egan, Wade and Shafran (2011)
10 Blankstein and Lumley (2015)
11 Affrunti and Woodruff-Borden (2014)
12 Park *et al.* (2015)
13 Boone, Claes and Luyten (2014)
14 Greenaway and Howlin (2010)
15 Fung (2009)
16 Conners *et al.* (1998)
17 Snaith (2015) and the World Health Organisation (2019)
18 Flett (2014)
19 Nauert (2014)
20 America: Miron *et al.* (2019); Australia: Longbottom (2016); New Zealand: McConnell (2016) and UK: Mohdin (2018)
21 Owen (2013)
22 Royal College of Paediatrics and Child Health (2015)

23 Törnblom, Werbart and Rydelius (2013)

24 Friedman (2006)

25 Sorotzkin (1998)

26 Albano, Chorpita and Barlow (2003)

27 Bolton *et al.* (2008)

28 Flett and Hewitt (2012)

29 DeSocio and Hootman (2004)

30 Cheney and colleagues (2014); Flett and Hewitt (2014)

31 Greenspon (2000, p.207)

32 Snaith (2015)

33 Fusun and Cemrenur (2014)

34 Comerchero (2008)

35 Burns (2015a)

36 BBC News (2015)

37 Snaith (2015)

38 Siegle and Schuler (2000)

39 Shafran and Mansell (2001, p.900)

40 e.g. Adelson and Wilson (2009); Burns (2008); Pett (2012)

41 Starley (2018)

42 Moon (2006)

43 Ratcliffe (2014)

44 Precey (2015)

45 Morris and Lomax (2014)

46 Neumeister (2004)

47 Hartley-Brewer (2015)

48 Bennathan, Boxall and Colley (1998, p.14)

49 Kunin (2017)

50 Mahnken (2017)

51 Manning (2017)

52 Atkinson *et al.* (1989)

53 Azevedo *et al.* (2010)

54 Kowal and Pritchard (1990)

55 Hewitt *et al.* (2002)

56 Öngen (2009)

57 e.g. Jowett *et al.* (2016); Lundh (2004); Wang, Yuen and Slaney (2009)

58 Flett and Hewitt (2014, p.899)

59 Chan (2009); Rice, Ashby and Gilman (2011)

60 Triggle (2015)

61 Cooke (2014)

62 Burns (2015b)

63 Whitworth (2015)

64 Udorie (2015)

65 Dour and Theran (2011); O'Connor, Rasmussen and Hawton (2010)

66 Cooke (2014)

67 Burns (2015a)

68 Booth (2016)

69 Buchanan (2015)

70 Flett and Hewitt (2014)

71 Mackinnon, Sherry and Pratt (2013)

72 Smith *et al.* (2017)

73 DfE (2014)

74 Snaith (2015)

75 e.g. *The Guardian* (2014)

76 Samaritans (2015); *The Times* (2015)

77 Afshar *et al.* (2011); Essau *et al.* (2008); O'Connor, Rasmussen and Hawton (2010)

78 e.g. Burgess (2015); Folksy (2014); Jackson (2004)

Chapter 1

What Is Perfectionism?

'Good enough is not good enough.'

'Perfectionist' is a term used by many to describe themselves and others, though whether they intend this as a compliment or insult depends on what they understand by 'perfectionism'.

It can mean different things to different people.

This is important, because what you understand 'perfectionism' to be will shape how you think about it, and therefore how you respond to it when you notice it in yourself or others.

- Do you use the term 'perfectionist'?
- What does it mean to you?
- Do you know whether other people share your understanding?

International research links perfectionism with high achievement, but also with school refusal, mental health issues and suicide.[1] If teachers and parents perceive perfectionism **positively**, they are likely to directly or indirectly reinforce it, potentially putting students at risk of mental ill health. If the same people view perfectionism **negatively**, they may behave in ways that challenge the young person to change. If done sensitively, using strategies such as those suggested in this book, this could result in positive change and enhanced emotional wellbeing for young people. However, encouraging someone to change can be a risky business, as we will discuss in later chapters.

This chapter will introduce you to a definition of perfectionism, areas of perfectionism, a consideration of what it is *not* as well as what it is, a discussion of how it is measured, observable behaviours, underlying thoughts and feelings linked with perfectionism, and its possible function as a coping mechanism for the young person. This chapter will also talk about the origin of perfectionism and what keeps it going, how common it is and what makes it more likely that someone will be high rather than low in perfectionism, or free from it at all. Finally, the chapter ends with links between perfectionism and other theories of learning and behaviour, and a range of case studies to bring to life what you have read.

A definition

There are many definitions of perfectionism in the international literature. For the purpose of this book, we will use the following:

> the overdependence of self-evaluation on the determined pursuit of personally demanding self-imposed standards in at least one highly salient domain, despite adverse consequences.[2]

In other words:

self-worth = achieving *at any cost*

By 'achieving', I mean getting what you are seeking – some kind of desired 'finished product'. There is no 'in between'. No partial self-worth from partial achievement. It therefore follows that:

Not achieving = 'I am worthless.'

This is an extreme, perhaps. But it lies at the heart of what it means to be a 'perfectionist'. This is the last time that phrase will be used in this book to describe a person, as I do not feel it is a helpful label. It conjures up the image of a specific type of person, with clearly defined and measurable traits, which is somewhat misleading. Instead, I will use the term **'high in perfectionism'**. It may feel slightly clumsier to read, but it keeps the individual firmly at the heart of discussions and their 'perfectionism' as something that can be changed rather than a fixed part of who they are. Our aim is not to label students, but to have a framework for better understanding them. Additionally, instead of 'worthless' I will use the less emotive term 'not good enough', as it feels somewhat easier to relate to and work with, and links well with the helpful phrase 'good enough', which plays a valuable role in child-rearing discussions across the legal, health and social systems.[3]

If the above summary sounds a bit extreme, perhaps it is worth considering perfectionism on a **continuum** (Figure 1.1), with individuals experiencing high, medium or low levels. This immediately brings a greater sense of flexibility to the situation, which is a key aspect of this book. Perfectionism shouts in 'black-or-white', all-or-nothing terms, and challenging it involves introducing the 'grey space' in between.

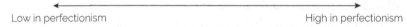

Low in perfectionism   High in perfectionism

FIGURE 1.1: PERFECTIONISM CONTINUUM

- Those with higher levels of perfectionism will experience the above definition at its most extreme; the most intense overdependence on self-evaluation, relentless pursuit of demanding standards and pervasive adverse consequences. For these individuals, perfectionism will have the biggest impact on their overall functioning and wellbeing. These may be the students struggling with or even refusing to begin a piece of work for fear of failing, or experiencing chronic headaches through over-working and under-resting. For these young people, high levels of perfectionism are likely to impair their academic potential and compromise their overall health.

- For those individuals lower in perfectionism, they will still experience an overdependence on self-evaluation, will still determinedly pursue personally demanding standards, and there will still be adverse consequences; however, this will be at a lower level of impairment to their functioning and wellbeing. These may be the students who spend a long time on their appearance in the mornings so that they look 'perfect', or who struggle to work in a group in case the other group members do not do things 'the right way'. For these young people, their perfectionism may cause them to perhaps be late sometimes or for others to think of them in less-than-helpful ways, but it is not going to have such a devastating effect on their overall development.

It is also worth noting that this is not a continuum on which everyone lies; those individuals not showing perfectionism would not be on this continuum at all. Perfectionism is something we want to move completely away from. Even those 'lower' in perfectionism are being driven by unhealthy attitudes and motivations, which do not typically respond well to the wider life challenges of adulthood. A more helpful continuum, on which we all reside, is introduced in Chapter 4.

Understanding perfectionism in terms of a continuum from low to high opens up a broader and more helpful discussion:

- Are people born a certain 'level' of perfectionism?

- Can people move up and down the spectrum?

- What does it look like to be high in perfectionism? How does it feel?

- What does it look like to be low in perfectionism? How does it feel?

- What causes someone to become higher in perfectionism?

- What helps them become lower?

- What **stops** them being lower? We will address this particular issue in Chapter 3.

- How might others respond to someone depending on where they are on the spectrum?

You may have your own ideas about the above questions. This book will seek to answer them using the available literature and psychological theory.

This book specifically considers perfectionism in our young people. For students high in perfectionism, achieving in something that is important to them is the root of their self-worth, even if there are negative outcomes associated with their attempts to achieve. Notice the above abbreviated definition states **'achieving'**, not 'achieved'.

This is an important distinction.

Some students may be high achievers in their area of value, and therefore have a reasonably positive sense of self-worth, however this is likely to be **fragile** as it relies on **continuing** to achieve.

Achieving is an attempt to make themselves feel calm and validated. They think in 'black-or-white' terms; either they are achieving, or they are not. Any sense of satisfaction (or more likely, relief) is short-lived as they must **continue** to achieve, to perform, to succeed. Past achievements and successes are dismissed as the continuous focus on current and future achievements takes precedence. Higher and higher standards are expected and a 'pursuit of perfect' appears to take place. Related beliefs about not showing weakness are likely to co-exist, leading to suppression of emotions in an attempt to present as ever-competent. A co-existing fear of failure is present and equally (if not more) motivating. An unrelenting and unsatisfying situation! Chapter 2 talks more about the adverse consequences of this way of living.

It is important to note that **this is all happening at an unconscious level**.

The individual is unlikely to be aware of the thoughts and feelings they are experiencing, and certainly not have quick access to the core belief about their self-worth. *These processes are taking place without the person knowing.* But they are nevertheless powerful and influence everything the person does.

Areas of life affected by perfectionism

'Influence everything the person does' may sound like another extreme statement, but perfectionism is about fixed thought patterns that shape the way an individual relates to the world around them. It is about a constant level of pressure being applied to themselves to perform in some way; being under constant pressure takes its toll on different areas of a young person's life.

- If they believe **'it is not okay to make mistakes'**, this is likely to affect many aspects of their day.

- If they believe they **'must not show emotions'**, this is likely to affect the way they approach learning situations and respond to relationships.

- If they believe they **'must always be achieving'**, it will be hard to 'switch off' and relax, leading to a range of physical and mental difficulties.

Some individuals may have all areas of their life affected by perfectionism, whereas others may only be affected in areas of particular value. Common areas include:

- **work/studies** (e.g. 'I have to get a particular mark'); NB if the individual is involved in sporting, artistic or musical pursuits instead or as well as academics, then these would also feature highly here

- **appearance/dress** (e.g. 'I have to look a certain way')

- **health/hygiene** (e.g. 'I have to be entirely clean/lean')

- **relationships** (e.g. 'I have to get the reaction I want')

- **organisation/order** (e.g. 'things have to be a certain way')

- **hobbies/leisure** (e.g. 'I have to be the best at this and do it perfectly')

- **written and/or spoken presentation** (e.g. 'I have to present myself my ideal way')

- **eating habits** (e.g. 'I have to eat only certain things at certain times')

- **time management/punctuality** (e.g. 'I have to be early').

It is perhaps apparent that the more areas affected by perfectionism, the more likely an individual will experience negative outcomes relating to this. Consider in particular the young person who applies a perfectionist attitude to their hobbies and relationships: this individual is unlikely to get any genuine relaxation in their lives, which would usually act as a buffer against the stresses and strains of the world.

How to spot a student high in perfectionism

This is something of a trick question! As previously explained, there is no 'set' person that fits the mould of 'perfectionist'. If I were to show you a classroom full of students, you may try and have a good guess at who is high in perfectionism – and most people are likely to choose a similar stereotype of young person: the conforming, hard-working, 'teacher's-pet' type of student, with the more disruptive and less engaged students definitely not being considered high in perfectionism – but ultimately much of what makes someone high in perfectionism is what is happening **under the surface**.

We will now look at some of the popular stereotypes and 'myths' about perfectionism before going on to explore ways in which we might identify a student high in perfectionism.

What perfectionism is not

There are many misconceptions about perfectionism which commonly get passed on from one person to another.

Let me take this opportunity to challenge the most popular of these:

- Perfectionism is **not** about actually *being* perfect, but about continually *seeking* perfection. Someone high in perfectionism may in fact believe they are not a 'perfectionist' because 'nothing they do is ever perfect'.

- Perfectionism is **not** the same as conscientiousness, or 'always trying one's best'. It may *look* similar, but the underlying driver and likely outcomes are very different.

- Perfectionism may **not** result in success and achievement. It is possible to be both successful and happy, though less likely if perfectionism is guiding behaviour rather than conscientiousness.

- Perfectionism is **not** just about academic work. It could be evident in any or all of a person's life.

- Perfectionism may be less about seeking achievement and more about avoiding failure, perhaps caused by an underlying fear of not being accepted or belonging, or inability to tolerate discomfort.

- Even if a student high in perfectionism *appears* confident and in control, this is likely to be fragile or a façade!

- Even if a student high in perfectionism appears to be succeeding, this is **not** satisfying or sustainable if driven by perfectionist beliefs.

Myths about perfectionism are explored further in Table 1.1.

Table 1.1: Perfectionism myths and reality

Perfectionism myths	Perfectionism reality
1. Students high in perfectionism are high achievers.	1. They may also be low-achievers due to fear of failure preventing them taking risks in their learning, or by their abilities not matching their high expectations.
2. Perfectionism is about academic work.	2. It may be evident in any or all areas of a person's life, not just academically.

3. Students high in perfectionism are confident in their ability and life is generally easy for them.	3. They are likely to lack confidence despite perhaps appearing outwardly confident. Many aspects of school and life present challenges to students high in perfectionism, depending on their areas of value.
4. Perfectionism is like a mental illness.	4. Perfectionism itself is not a mental illness but may contribute to mental illness.
5. Perfectionism comes largely from upbringing, but being a 'non-perfectionist' is just who you are.	5. Perfectionism arises from and is maintained by a combination of factors, as is being a 'non-perfectionist'.
6. Students high in perfectionism will go on to do well in life.	6. They might not necessarily go on to do well and achieve and in fact may experience poor health and failure in different life areas.
7. Students high in perfectionism should just 'let it go'.	7. They may need external support to challenge their perfectionist thoughts; this may not be as simple as 'letting it go' but there may be clear small steps towards this that schools and families can implement.
8. There is a stereotypical student who is high in perfectionism.	8. No two students high in perfectionism are entirely alike; all are unique individuals with their own profile of strength and needs.
9. Perfectionism is just the way you are.	9. It can change! People are made up of many more elements than just their perfectionism.
10. Even though it may cause stress, it is generally better to be high in perfectionism than not.	10. There is some confusion between perfectionism and conscientiousness. A certain level of stress is good for performance, but not too much.
11. There's nothing anyone can really do to help change a student high in perfectionism.	11. We can target certain skills and needs to help someone high in perfectionism change.
12. Change is hard, so students high in perfectionism will probably only change if something drastic happens in their life.	12. Early intervention may help to prevent perfectionism becoming stronger and more ingrained. We do not want to wait for something significant to happen to the young person as this may be very serious.

Are any of these surprising? It may be worth reflecting on what you believe about perfectionism and considering how this may have shaped your behaviours to date, towards both yourself and others. Consider in particular how key adults believing some of the myths above may reinforce perfectionism in young people.

Here are some examples of scenarios caused by high levels of perfectionism that would not be the usual 'stereotype':

- 'If I don't try, I can't fail' resulting in disengagement and work refusal.

- 'I need to check my hair still looks good', resulting in distraction, leaving the classroom, using a phone camera during lessons, not allowing staff to remove their mobile phone.

- 'How can I score even more goals than ever before in tonight's match?', leading to distraction and poor focus in class, coming in late to lessons and homework incomplete as time is spent practicing football skills and hours are spent watching internet video clips of football.

- 'I have to practise that violin piece again as soon as I get home', resulting in feigned illness to leave school, irritability with adults, desire to rush and finish work quickly.

- 'I'm a failure', resulting in disruptive behaviour to reinforce the point.

- 'I can't believe I said that to him, what a stupid thing to say', resulting in low concentration, using a phone in class, talking with peers rather than focusing on the lesson, leaving lessons.

- 'No one makes me look like an idiot', leading to aggression and exclusion.

How do you measure perfectionism?

So if we cannot identify a student high in perfectionism simply by looking at them, and we want to avoid falling into the trap of stereotyping, how do we identify those students high in perfectionism?

Some behaviours *may* give us an indication that a student is experiencing perfectionism, however the identification of this is only really possible through knowing their thoughts and feelings. How do you measure these?

There are six popular rating scales in use for 'measuring' perfectionism,[4] which have some consensus about the following aspects of someone rating highly in perfectionism, with examples given under each:

- **high standards or expectations**

  - I set higher goals than most people

  - I am very good at focusing my efforts on attaining a goal.

- **criticism of self or others**

  - I demand nothing less than perfect of myself

  - other people disappoint me.

- **negative automatic thoughts**

  - I cannot achieve what I need to do

  - this will be too hard for me.

- **concerns or doubts**

  - I usually have doubts about the simple everyday things I do

  - it takes me a long time to do something right.

- **sensitivity to mistakes**

  - if I fail at work/school, I am a failure as a person

  - I hate being less than the best at things.

Some scales highlight parental expectations (e.g. my parents set very high standards for me; my family expects me to be perfect),[5] parental criticism (e.g. I am punished for doing things less than perfectly; my parents never try to understand my mistakes)[6] and organisation (e.g. organisation is very important to me; I am a neat person).[7]

American educational psychologists Adelson and Wilson (2009) describe five different 'types' of students high in perfectionism:

- Academic Achievers

- Aggravated Accuracy Assessors

- Risk Evaders

- Controlling Image Managers

- Procrastinating Perfectionists.

Perhaps you can think of young people who may fit each of these descriptors?

The measurement of perfectionism is in fact highly problematic and there is no specific 'tool' available for doing this reliably. International research studies typically use self-rating questionnaires with questions or statements such as 'Have you felt a failure as a person because you have not succeeded in meeting your goals?',[8] 'I find it difficult to meet others' expectations of me'[9] and 'I get upset when things don't go as planned.'[10]

**If you were high in perfectionism,
how might you answer these?**

There is a high likelihood that you would want to avoid feeling any sense of incompetence, perceived weakness or lack of control. You would therefore be unlikely to answer these with full honesty. This 'social desirability bias' is particularly strong for people high in perfectionism,[11] so this is a major problem with self-rating scales.

Perfectionism is also included as a measure in rating scales for other areas of interest in children, such as in the measurement of dysfunctional attitudes, eating disorders, and routines and anxiety.

These rely less on the individual rating themselves, and more on their key adults reflecting on observable behaviours.

So let's consider observable behaviours. This is the 'easiest' way to try and identify high levels of perfectionism as they are right there in front of you, communicating loudly and clearly. As approached above, some stereotypical behaviours of a student high in perfectionism could be:

- attention to detail, precision and accuracy

- organised

- neat

- high levels of concentration and focus

- drive and ambition shown through dedication and pursuit of success

- hard worker

- high expectations shown through comments and actions.

If you look over that list again but this time with the lens of 'healthy learner', you will note that the two coincide. Therefore, the above behaviours alone are not symptomatic of perfectionism. In fact, some students high in perfectionism may not demonstrate these at all! However, if you ask anyone to describe a 'perfectionist', I imagine that at least a couple of behaviours in this list will come up in their answer. It is a common stereotype and, as you will see in Chapter 3, something that can make change very challenging indeed.

More concerning and problematic behaviours that better indicate high levels of perfectionism as distinct from 'healthy learning' are as follows:

- excessive organising and list-making, including arranging their environment

- difficulty making decisions

- repeating and correcting

- overcompensating

- excessive checking and reassurance-seeking

- procrastination, perhaps leading to work being handed in late or incomplete

- not knowing when to quit, e.g. spend many hours editing work, training excessively

- giving up too soon

- excessive slowness

- spending a lot of time staying behind after school

- failure to delegate or to ask for help

- hoarding

- high discrepancy between their aspirations and their performance

- avoidance, e.g. last-minute cancellations, work refusals, 'defiance', spending a lot of time alone, avoiding entering competitions

- reluctance to speak in front of the class, perhaps appearing very shy

- attempting to change the behaviour of others

- restricting eating, increasing exercise (perhaps training for longer or harder than recommended), spending time applying and checking make-up/hair

- rehearsing jokes and stories, high level of upset if feel they have not come across as clever or funny

- excessive or surprising level of upset by tasks/situations that could be perceived by others as achievable/manageable, e.g. a regular mistake, or transition

- appear to be coping well in the face of multiple and excessive pressure (e.g. exam time, music performance, sport tournament, illness, family issues, etc.).[12]

Please note, we all display some of these behaviours some of the time! Perfectionism is about the *degree* of these behaviours.

- We need to be concerned if they are becoming **compulsive**, i.e. the student appears to no longer have a choice about what they are doing, but rather appears compelled to do things.

- Our concern should also be triggered if these behaviours appear to be affecting a person's **functioning** (i.e. reducing the quality of their schoolwork, social relationships, health, self-care or independence).

When considering a student's behaviours, we are building up a picture of them over time and across different situations. If there are some or many of these behaviours present for a lot of their school-/home-life then perhaps we may start to wonder if they have high levels of perfectionism.

Table 1.2 summarises the behaviours that may give insights into perfectionist thoughts and feelings held by the young person.

Table 1.2: Behaviours suggesting a high level of perfectionism

Behaviour	What this might look like
Compulsive behaviours	The student seems to be responding to an irresistible urge; they may struggle not to do something even if you intervene, e.g. checking, organising, reassurance-seeking, controlling others...
Avoidance behaviours	The student is successfully escaping something that may be causing anxiety, e.g. by procrastinating, repeated starting over, resisting attempts to have 'personal' or 'emotional' discussions, refusal to speak in front of the class, giving up too soon or refusing to start, isolating themselves...
Surprising over-reactions	The student responds in ways that feel out of proportion to the trigger, e.g. making a mistake, not understanding, forgetting something for a lesson, a comment from a peer, plans being changed at the last minute...

cont.

Behaviour	What this might look like
Signs of stress	The student appears tense, tired, distracted, irritable, complains of physical aches and pains, is absent...
Apparently coping well	The student seemingly 'under-reacts' to events that would typically cause some visible distress, including facing multiple pressures. This is likely to be a superficial façade in which the young person feels they need to present as coping, competent and in control at all times.
Excessiveness	The student spends a long time and a lot of energy on things that are out of proportion to what is required, they do not 'know when to quit', they are likely to over-rehearse, stay behind after class, complete lots of homework, etc.

Let us now consider the underlying perfectionist thoughts and feelings that may be driving the above behaviours.

Thoughts

You can try to identify how a young person might be thinking by listening to some of the things they are saying, looking at what they write or draw about, or considering who they might be being influenced by. Some examples of perfectionist thoughts are:

- I should be a size 6 and wear make-up to look good (appearance/'aesthetic performance').

- I need to seem clever and funny to everyone I meet (social performance).

- I must be 100 per cent sure (checking).

- I need to always get over 90 per cent (academic performance).

- I can't play a note wrong (musical performance).

- I have to train harder so I can be the best (sporting performance).

- Things have to be in the right order; I need to make more lists (order and organisation).

Table 1.3 describes the 'cognitive errors' related to perfectionism.

Table 1.3: Cognitive errors in perfectionism

Cognitive error	Description	Example
Catastrophising	Expecting the worst, no matter what	If I make a mistake on this something really bad might happen like someone might even die!
Filtering	Magnifying the negative details and 'filtering out' the more positive aspects	I made three mistakes, I can't believe it, they were such stupid errors.
Over-generalising	Coming to a general conclusion based on a single piece of evidence	I didn't get the highest in the class; I'm a failure.
Global labelling	Extreme form of generalising; taking one or two qualities and using them as a negative global judgement of self or others	I failed that test so I'm a failure.
Jumping to conclusions	Assuming we know what the outcome was/will be	I'm gonna fail; they thought I was stupid.
Personalising	Taking everything personally and comparing self to others	She was rude to me because she thinks I'm not bright enough to be here.
Control fallacies, in particular:	Believing we are victims of fate OR responsible for everything	
blaming	Holding others responsible for our pain OR blaming ourselves for every problem	I wouldn't be so stressed if I was better at this; it's your fault I'm stressed.
fallacy of fairness	Resenting that others do not share our views of fairness; refusing to believe life is not fair	He did not deserve to win that, that's not fair.
fallacy of change	Expecting people to change to suit us	I'm going to keep on doing it like this and you need to deal with it.
Heaven's reward fallacy	Expecting reward for sacrifice and bitter when it does not come	I worked hard, I deserve better.

cont.

Cognitive error	Description	Example
'Shoulds'	Ironclad rules which result in guilt, anger, frustration, resentment	I should be doing as much work as possible, I should be liked all the time.
Emotional reasoning	Assuming our feelings are true reflections of how things are	I am stressed so this is a stressful task.
Always being right	Continually having to prove self right, no matter what the cost, including being defensive and finding faults in others	I can't make mistakes so you must be wrong.
Selective abstraction	Taking one detail and believing this while ignoring everything else in the context	The whole concert was ruined because of my one mistake.
Dichotomous thinking	Black-or-white', 'all-or-nothing'; there is no middle ground	I am either the best or I am a failure.
Rumination, including: concern over mistakes difficulty accepting the past	Focusing attention on the symptoms of distress, what caused it and its consequences	I said that stupid thing then they looked disgusted; I'm such an idiot. I got that so wrong, I wonder who noticed? I can't believe I did that.
Worry, including: self-doubt fear of failure or negative social evaluations perceived inability to consistently meet high standards	A feeling of anxiety about actual or potential problems	I can't fit enough revision in to do well enough on this test; I'm going to fail. I'm not up to this. They will think I'm stupid. I can't do it.
Disconnection and rejection schema, likely to result in: negative perceptions of school and family relationships perceived discrimination	Fixed patterns of thinking that others will not reliably provide social connection and emotional support	They won't be there when I need them, they will leave me to help someone else. No one cares, or understands everyone is too busy for me, there is nobody like me. They only do that because I'm a girl/ethnic minority/ from a poor background/ gay.

A fixed mindset	Difficulties viewing ability as changeable and a tendency to focus on the end point rather than the journey	People are either clever or they are not. The goal is the most important thing, I'm not interested in progress and effort.
Setting high personal standards	Having goals and aspirations that are particularly elevated	I will get the best anyone has ever done in this project/race/concert. I will look flawless at all times.

The last point in Table 1.3 is an interesting one. You might ask, 'How do I know if a young person's standards are high in a helpful way, or perfectionistic?' Here are some questions you could consider about what the student is currently focused on:

- What is the young person expecting for the outcome?

- What level of effort do they expect to have to put in?

- Are their standards higher than those of peers?

- Is the student able to meet those standards?

- Would they be very upset if they did not meet those standards?

- Do their standards help them achieve their goals or do they get in the way?

- What would be the costs to the young person of relaxing a particular standard or ignoring a self-imposed 'rule'?

- What would be the benefits to the young person of relaxing a particular standard or ignoring a self-imposed 'rule'?

In other words, are the young person's standards **unreasonably** high, such that the individual can never be 'good enough'?

One way of considering those students of concern is to consider a 'discrepancy model'. This highlights the 'discrepancy' between a student's expectations and their actual achievement or performance level. This can be seen in Figure 1.2. The students of most concern are those for whom their expectations greatly outweigh their actual performance.

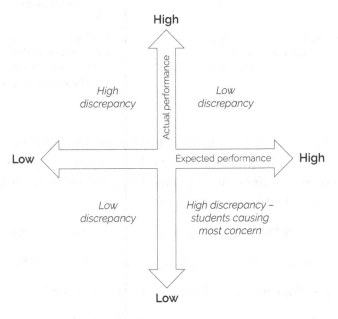

FIGURE 1.2: DISCREPANCY MODEL

The important thing to note is that self-esteem is based upon the 'actual' outcome compared with the 'expected' outcome. A student high in perfectionism is likely to have high expectations – not a bad thing in and of itself. However, if their *actual* performance does not measure up, their self-esteem will suffer. If their actual performance *does* measure up, their self-esteem remains intact; however, it will be fragile, as discussed previously, as it relies on *continued* successful outcomes.

Feelings

You can try to identify what a young person might be feeling by noticing how you feel when you are around them (signs of projection, transference and counter-transference),[13] watching their behaviour, listening to things they say, reflecting on things they write/draw and considering how you might feel in their position. Some examples of feelings you might notice are:

- tension

- anxiety

- fear

- frustration

- stress.

This may be a good point at which to highlight that these feelings are not negative in and of themselves. All emotions exist to give us important messages about our experiences and to keep us safe. Stress, in particular, can help us to perform when needed. However, too much stress can result in the opposite: poor performance, as our brains tend to 'shut down' when they become overloaded with stress. Too much of any emotion can lead to bigger problems. More concerning feelings linked with perfectionism include distress and exhaustion.

Now we have considered the typical sorts of thoughts, feelings and behaviours of someone high in perfectionism, would you think any differently about the classroom of students mentioned earlier? Who are the students who may fly under the radar but may actually be very high in perfectionism?

Who would be your priority for support?

Where does perfectionism come from?

It is not known for sure.

It may be something babies are born with a 'vulnerability' to develop, they may inherit 'tendencies' from their parents, or it may be developed through messages learned from their environment (home, school, the media, society as a whole). These are briefly described on the following pages, concluding with the popular current theory this book is based upon.

Theory 1: Parenting

In particular, a 'pushy' or 'demanding' style of parenting has been linked with high levels of perfectionism. This can include an authoritarian approach, parents with high levels of perfectionism themselves, harsh expectations and greater focus on performance rather than learning, and on product and achievement over process and progress. Interestingly, research has suggested that students high in perfectionism often perceive this theory to be a cause of their perfectionism.[14] This theory links with the popular culture titles 'stage mother', 'tiger mother', 'helicopter parent' and 'Kyōiku Mama' ('education mother' in Japanese), all of which have links with anxiety, depression and suicide in young people. Infants and young children interpret the world based on very limited information and understanding, so their conclusions may not accurately reflect what was intended. Unclear communication and non-expression of emotion can further reinforce such unhelpful beliefs and create very fixed attitudes about what is expected.

Theory 2: Attachment

This relational perspective highlights the interactive influence of the child and carer through the emotional bonding process. The emotional attunement of the carer towards the infant is crucial for developing a secure attachment. An infant learns who they are and what they can expect from other people and the world around them from their early interactions with their primary caregiver. Where an infant cannot rely upon a consistent supply of love, comfort, affection and their needs being met without fear, confusion or anxiety, they are likely to develop an insecure attachment style as a way to stay physically and emotionally safe in their environment. An insecure attachment style has strong links in the research with perfectionism.[15] Infants and young children can learn to suppress their emotions and to try to behave 'perfectly' to ensure a more consistent and predictable response from their caregivers. This can continue as their way of coping with relationships and be seen in their school behaviour.

Theory 3: Intergenerational transmission

This suggests that perfectionism is in the genes. There is not much support for this theory, other than perhaps a biological vulnerability towards perfectionism; for example, as suggested in the eating disorder literature. Some researchers believe perfectionism is a distinct personality trait,[16] whereas others note it to be just associated with certain personality traits, for example with 'neuroticism'. Where parents and their children display high levels of perfectionism, it is then of course challenging to determine how much is genetic and how much is learned. Until a 'perfectionism gene' is discovered (and let's hope it is not, as it may make change feel even more challenging), this theory is not considered to be particularly helpful.

Theory 4: Cognitive processes

This theory suggests that perfectionism is a set of beliefs trigger-ing a thought process in which self-worth is based upon critical self-evaluation. Triggers in the environment, such as the attitudes and behaviour of key adults or the cultural expectations of a school, interact with a person's core schemas to mediate the development of perfectionist beliefs. The individual's coping strategies in response to their environment are therefore grounded in and maintained by the faulty core belief about the self: 'I am what I achieve',[17] resulting in unrealistic expectations and a 'self-destructive double-bind'.[18] The majority of intervention research has focused on this theory as it relies heavily on cognitive-behavioural approaches, targeting unhelpful behaviours and their related underlying thought processes.

Theory 5: The environment

This includes the influence of siblings, peers, the school academic environment, the wider cultural influence and trauma. It may be that comparison of themselves with (possibly high-performing?)

siblings or peers may reflect an attempt by students to meet indirect parental or teacher expectations.[19] Bould (2016) suggested that eating disorders amongst teenage girls may result from perfectionistic traits arising from aspirational schools encouraging girls to *try their best at all times*. Boone and colleagues (2012) found that 'state' perfectionism could be induced in UK university students irrespective of their levels of 'trait' perfectionism, offering further support for this theory.

Another way of thinking about perfectionism

It is the interaction of the above theories that is most helpful in understanding someone's perfectionism. Current thinking in the area suggests that it is probable that a combination of the above factors make it more or less likely that an individual will experience high levels of perfectionism. Although it may feel simpler and easier to have one thing to 'blame' or consider, again this is not the real world. Perfectionism is more complex than that, and to truly challenge it effectively we need to take into account all the above possibilities.

However, rather than looking for something or someone to 'blame' or attempting to hold in mind all the above factors, it may be more helpful to think about the **function** of the perfectionist behaviours and then try to focus on the corresponding **underlying unmet need**.

If behaviour is considered a form of communication that tells us something about a person's needs, then perfectionist behaviours may be conceptualised as communicating something about the student's needs.

Maslow (1970) described a hierarchy of human needs which it is believed that all individuals will be seeking to meet through their behaviours, starting from the base of the pyramid and working their way up. As seen in Figure 1.3, our most basic biological needs must be met first, including our physical comfort level which incorporates our sensory needs (i.e. feedback through our visual, auditory, olfactory, tactile, vestibular and proprioceptive systems).

Following these needs being met, we seek to feel emotionally secure by having consistent and nurturing responses from others. After this is met, we can seek out our social belonging needs and try to find the place we fit in. Once met, we can pursue our self-esteem and feel good about the things we do and who we are, followed by achieving our potential through balancing all aspects of ourselves in our environment. When a need is not met, the individual will experience a level of anxiety which motivates them to meet the need.

FIGURE 1.3: MASLOW'S HIERARCHY OF HUMAN NEEDS

We are all seeking to be the best we can be.
Not having a need met feels unpleasant.

In this way, we can think of perfectionism as being a coping mechanism for managing the anxiety created from an underlying unmet biological/sensory/neurological, emotional, social or self-esteem need. This is known as the 'Iceberg model' in that the behaviours we see 'above the surface' are indicative of deeper issues happening 'beneath the surface' (Figure 1.4). For any of these functions it appears that perfectionism is a behaviour designed to *calm* the individual in the short term, by trying to reduce the anxiety from an unmet need. However, it is more likely to perpetuate anxiety, therefore it is largely an unhelpful coping mechanism in the long term.

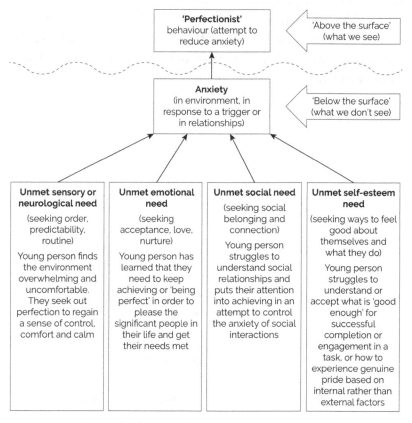

FIGURE 1.4: ICEBERG MODEL OF UNDERLYING NEEDS

This approach allows us to focus on the root causes that lead to perfectionist behaviours. Targeting these root causes is more likely to bring about lasting change than what has more traditionally been tried: trying to alter behaviours or cognitive processes without addressing underlying unmet needs.

How do I know what the underlying need is?

Sometimes it may be obvious, other times you may need to do some more investigation. Some suggestions are shown in the below boxes in Figure 1.5. If you follow the arrows, they lead to the respective areas for intervention for each underlying need.

Sensory or neurological need	**Emotional need**	**Social need**	**Self-esteem need**
Does the student appear to be overwhelmed or overstimulated at certain times of the day or in certain environments? Do they struggle with unstructured times or managing unexpected changes? Do they respond well to having set routines and predictable activities? Do they engage in any self-stimulating or self-soothing sensory activities?	Does the student often try to please you or gain your approval? Do they frequently seek reassurance? Do they avoid getting close to people, including discussing personal or emotional matters? Do they seem reluctant or unable to share any concerns or weaknesses? Do they seem to be presenting themselves as competent, coping and in control even though they may be under significant pressure?	Does the student have a lack of close or meaningful friendships? Do they spend more time with adults, younger students or alone than with same-age peers? Do they sometimes behave in unusual ways and/or appear to not understand what is expected in social interactions? Do they imitate others? Do they have an unhealthy relationship with social media?	Does the student appear to get relief from a finished product rather than enjoying the journey to get there? Do they struggle to accept praise? Do they make the same mistakes repeatedly, get frustrated but seem unable to change, despite prompting and encouragement? Do they describe themselves in 'black-or-white' and 'catastrophic' terms?

School: Make the environment as predictable as possible, minimise changes and prepare the student well for upcoming changes, use visual supports, provide sensory breaks. **Student:** Learn sensory coping strategies and anxiety management.	**School:** Provide a 'key person', teach emotional literacy skills, give opportunities to explore and express feelings. **Student:** Learn coping strategies, including assertiveness, mindfulness and self-acceptance.	**School:** Teach social thinking skills, provide opportunities to interact with positive role models, have clear and proactive bullying and social media policies. **Student:** Learn coping strategies, including communication skills.	**School:** Use a CBT approach to challenge underlying thoughts, promote positive self-esteem using growth mindset culture. **Student:** Learn coping strategies, including thought-challenging.

FIGURE 1.5: FUNCTION OF THE PERFECTIONISM
AND IDEAS FOR WHAT TO DO TO HELP

What keeps perfectionism going?

So why does perfectionism continue, even if there are 'adverse consequences'?

Perfectionism is a trap.

Cognitive-behavioural theory can help us understand this better, as shown in Figure 1.6:

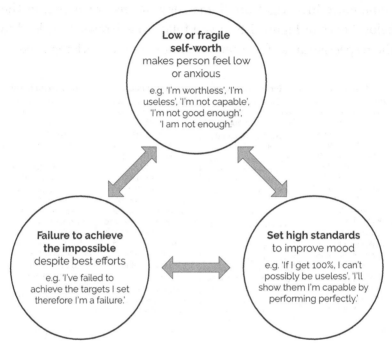

FIGURE 1.6: COGNITIVE-BEHAVIOURAL CYCLE OF PERFECTIONISM

Not achieving – even the slightest perception of this – creates the automatic thought, 'I am not good enough.' This thought of not being good enough creates deeply unpleasant feelings, which the person will seek to avoid as no one likes to 'sit' with uncomfortable feelings. So any sign that the individual is **not** achieving is likely to create great anxiety for them as it will trigger their underlying fear that 'I am not good enough.'

As long as they are achieving, their self-worth is maintained. They are avoiding that uncomfortable place of 'worthlessness'. As long as they are seeking achievement, they are avoiding failure. However, because they are constantly seeking achievement, they are constantly fighting the thought 'I am not good enough', as any achievement is only temporary and needs replicating again and again. The cycle continues.

With such exhausting mental processes taking place, how can the student have space to take on 'real' challenges? They often opt for things they know they will be successful in, or if they do take on 'real' challenges, the standards they set for themselves are so high they cannot possibly be met or maintained; both these scenarios reinforce the underlying belief 'I am not good enough.' Figure 1.6 shows this cycle and how it keeps itself going, resulting in a 'trap' for the individual.

This cognitive-behavioural explanation is a popular way to understand what keeps perfectionism going. Chapter 3 addresses other ways in which perfectionism is maintained.

How common is perfectionism?

Many people describe themselves as perfectionists,[20] but prevalence of perfectionism, particularly within school children, is difficult to ascertain for a number of reasons, some of which relate to the issue of defining perfectionism. Another reason is the bias that it is predominantly Higher Education students that are included in research, rather than school children. This misses out those students who do not go on to Higher Education, perhaps as a direct result of high levels of perfectionism, and therefore perhaps the ones most needing to 'be researched', as these could be the most vulnerable young people.

Another reason that it is challenging to ascertain how many children and young people have high levels of perfectionism is the use of self-rating scales to identify participants and their related 'level' of perfectionism. As described above, the social desirability bias[21] is likely to be particularly high amongst this population, meaning self-rating information may be next to useless. The use of different rating scales also makes measuring perfectionism rates challenging, since different assessment tools reflect different conceptualisations of perfectionism and therefore cannot be assumed to be 'measuring' the same thing. The use of alternative 'measures' such as parent or teacher reports, and exploration of individuals' unique experiences of perfectionism are rare, reflecting a positivist assumption about the nature of perfectionism (i.e. that it is a real, measurable 'thing' that is the same across everyone).

Despite these difficulties with knowing exactly how 'common' perfectionism really is, a simple internet search of perfectionism reveals the claim on a variety of websites that 'approximately 30% of the general population suffers from perfectionism',[22] with the suggestion that this is as high as 87 per cent in the 'gifted population',[23] 30 per cent of this figure being 'neurotic'. It is fair to say there is neither quality evidence to corroborate *nor* dispute these claims. The basis of this book works on the premise that even if *some* of our students are experiencing perfectionism then it is worth addressing.

What makes it more likely someone will be high in perfectionism?

Some researchers believe girls are more likely to be high in perfectionism than boys,[24] however others find no difference in gender.[25] Affluence has been associated with negative effects of perfectionism in academically-gifted American youth,[26] and a non-approving home environment is likely to contribute greatly.[27] A person's race has been explored, with no conclusive findings.[28] Perhaps more helpfully, we can look at what makes it more likely someone will be *low* in perfectionism. Various factors appear to play an important role in making it less likely a person will show high levels of perfectionism. These 'protective' factors against perfectionism include:

- self-worth[29]

- self-efficacy[30]

- self-esteem[31]

- self-control[32]

- resilience,[33] including specific coping resources, competencies and capabilities[34]

- locus of control[35]

- growth mindset,[36] positive mindset,[37] or good-enough mindset[38]

- a nurturing and cohesive home environment with direct expression of expectations and encouragement.[39]

Links with theory

Perfectionism has links with other theories with which you may be familiar and which you may have considered in what you have read so far. These related theories are briefly addressed here:

Mindsets[40]

Perfectionism relates to a **'fixed mindset'**, with rigid ways of thinking and behaving that focus mainly on the outcome rather than the process. A fixed mindset has very low tolerance for mistakes (which are seen as signs of failure), effort (which is seen as a sign of not being good enough) and emotion (which is seen as an interference and intolerable weakness). This is the opposite of a **'growth mindset'** which believes in the value of effort, making mistakes, and using emotional information to help us achieve success and happiness.

Learning goals[41]

Perfectionism has links with **performance (or achievement)** goals in which the individual's focus and motivation is driven by the end product. This is the opposite of **process-oriented, mastery or learning** goals which value the journey as well as the destination, to encourage deeper and longer-lasting learning, a more positive and balanced self-image, and likelihood of future success.

Self-determination theory[42]

Perfectionism links with the **self-determination theory** of learning in terms of the motivation behind choices made, regardless of external factors. It is believed that people will function and grow if their three innate psychological needs are met with support from the social environment: competence, relatedness and autonomy. Someone high in perfectionism may experience threats to each of these factors if they doubt their own ability, lack meaningful connection with others and do not feel in control of their life.

Locus of control[43]

Perfectionism relates to extreme ends of the locus of control: either believing that oneself should have total control over everything that happens, or believing that oneself has no control whatsoever. Ideally, a person would have a healthy balance of the two.

Hierarchy of need[44]

Students high in perfectionism may have their focus on striving to do things perfectly rather than achieving '**self-actualisation**', hence they are perhaps trying to meet a more basic motivational need of security, belonging or self-esteem. This may be overlooked as they may *appear* competent, capable and in control.

Defence mechanisms[45]

It may be that perfectionism develops as an avoidance-oriented coping mechanism,[46] as suggested in a correlation between perfectionism and survivors of childhood sexual abuse.[47] This fits with the idea of perfectionism functioning as a way of managing anxiety arising from an unmet need. While perfectionism, or the 'target' of the perfectionism (studies, appearance, etc.) is the focus, the unmet need can remain unexamined. This may be beneficial when a person is likely to experience great distress during the recognition of their underlying needs.

Case study examples

If all of this feels a bit abstract, don't worry!

Let's explore some case study examples to bring to life some of the theory discussed above. These case studies are amalgamations of real-life students, families and school staff I have worked with over my time in mental health services and education, with individual identities protected. For each case study I have suggested the areas of perfectionism for the young person and the possible underlying need to be explored further. Here are some questions for you to consider as you read:

- Do you recognise anyone you know in these accounts?

- What are your 'gut feelings' about these students?

- Who would you be most worried about?

- Do the possible underlying needs surprise you?

- Are there are young people you know who you might think about differently after reading about Amelia, Charlie, Mia and Harrison?

Case study 1: Amelia

Amelia is a bright teenage girl, for whom learning has always appeared to come easily. She frequently gets the highest mark in class and always has her homework in on time, completed to a very high standard. She is a member of many of the school sports teams and plays in the school orchestra. Amelia is the first to audition for school plays, in which she always gets a lead role and for which she rehearses every spare minute at home. She volunteers in school community projects and is always very neat and presentable.

The school is relying on her to score highly in her final examinations and present the ideal image of the school when local news reporters visit. They expect her to go on to be Head Girl and eventually get into an elite university. They have no concerns about Amelia. Amelia has no concerns about herself. Achievement is important to her, and she is doing well. Success takes focus and determination; she has these qualities so does not need help from anyone. The only area of the curriculum in which Amelia does not excel is Art; she does not care about this as she finds it an 'unfair' subject in which someone can produce what looks like a scribble and it be worth millions.

Amelia has no true friendships. She gets along superficially with everyone, however other students find her achievements annoying as she often suggests that you either have talent or you don't, and never seems genuinely pleased when others succeed. She is not around to socialise in or out of school as she is so busy, and wouldn't know what to do anyway if anyone was upset or needed advice. The things she says and does make people think she wouldn't like them if they were overweight, did not wear makeup, or were a bit messy, so people like this generally keep their distance. Amelia has never had a deep or meaningful friendship, so to her this does not feel like a problem: isn't this what everyone experiences? She gets along with everyone so what is the issue? Amelia finds emotions like anger, sadness and fear highly inconvenient and pushes these away successfully through keeping very busy, restricting her diet (she calls it 'eating clean') and doing high levels of exercise until she cannot feel anymore. With feelings out of the way she can focus better on the next thing on her to-do list. She has heard that A-Levels are much harder than GCSEs, but that was probably from people who weren't very clever; she doesn't think she will have any difficulty.

Areas of perfectionism: work/studies, appearance/dress, health/ hygiene, presentation, eating habits. Amelia appears to have a lot of areas of her life affected by perfectionism.

Possible underlying need: cognitive errors. Amelia shows signs of a 'fixed mindset' and very definite 'rules' she lives her life by. Although she is making these ways of thinking work for her currently in terms of being widely successful, she is likely to find difficulties with these when out 'in the real world' including in Higher Education, where she is likely to experience greater challenge. It may be that she also has underlying needs in social communication and emotion regulation that could benefit from some support.

Case study 2: Charlie

Charlie is a primary school pupil who is frequently being described as a 'natural' at anything he tries. He is reliably successful in all areas of the curriculum and is chosen as team captain whenever there is group-work, particularly in PE in which he truly shines. Charlie takes part in lots of extracurricular sport clubs to help 'channel his talents'; these take up the majority of his evenings and weekends so although he doesn't always get his homework done, he is getting involved with lots of high-flying clubs. Charlie is very well-liked by his peers. Sporting success is very important to Charlie; he uses every free moment at school to practise football with his friends. They love him being on their team as he is a top goalscorer. This makes him feel good about himself.

Charlie has been spotted by his teachers 'cheating' on class tests by looking at the work of the person next to him. They can't understand this as they know Charlie knows the answers. They are also confused that sometimes he does not want to enter the competitions they arrange yet they know that he would likely win, even in sport. He appears embarrassed when they invite him up to the front of school in assembly to congratulate him on yet another brilliant achievement and occasionally can be quite defiant about not wanting to go into assembly, finding lots of reasons to stay in the classroom instead. His parents are confused by this, along with Charlie's sullen behaviour at home in which he rarely wants to spend time with them and would rather play on his computer games, pursuing the best scores for his age group online. He can get quite irritable and tense with them. They are worried he will waste his 'natural talents' by not working hard enough. They and his teachers are keen to dissuade him from his dream job of professional footballer, as they think he should do something much more sensible and 'intelligent'.

Areas of perfectionism: work/studies, hobbies/leisure. Charlie appears to have a couple of key areas of his life affected by perfectionism, which seem to be becoming more of an issue as he gets older. There is a combination here of areas valued more by him, and areas valued more by the key adults in his life.

Possible underlying need: self-esteem and social belonging. Charlie appears to be seeking out a sense of belonging in his peer group, and trying to find ways to feel good about himself in areas that are important to him. For Charlie, this is appearing as rejecting of some of the things that are important to the key adults in his life. It is important that Charlie finds ways to 'fit in' with a supportive social group while also doing things that make him feel genuinely good about himself. It will be helpful to understand what Charlie expects for himself, and what he thinks others expect from him in terms of his education, so that he can truly feel a sense of self-worth and engage wholeheartedly in his learning.

Case study 3: **Mia**

Mia is a primary school pupil whose parents and school staff describe as 'away with the fairies'. She is considered to be 'low average' at school in terms of her abilities and often just blends in with the other children. Mia keeps her belongings in her school bag which is hung on a peg in the cloakroom. Mia checks her bag after every lesson to make sure everything is in the right compartment. She is not allowed to do this so she 'tricks' the teacher by asking to go to the toilet, which is next to the cloakroom. The teacher is often irritated she goes to the toilet so much but Mia doesn't care as it means she gets to check her bag. She feels calm when she knows everything is where it is supposed to be. During lessons Mia focuses on her pencil case and its contents, taking them out and putting them back in, in a particular order. If anyone interrupts her she frowns at them and starts again. Sometimes she has been heard to growl when she seems particularly frustrated at her order being disrupted. Mia often misses the teacher's instructions because of this checking and organising, but has learned to copy what the person next to her does.

Mia came to the teacher's attention once when she had what school described as a 'meltdown' in which she screamed, pushed another child over and hid under a table clutching her belongings. Another child had reportedly gone into her bag and Mia had found this unbearable. Mia's parents were not concerned; they describe her as 'a bit weird' compared to her five siblings but they are happy as long as she is not getting in as much trouble as they did at school. A teaching assistant in Mia's class has noticed that when getting changed for PE, Mia can be very slow as she takes a lot of time over doing things in a particular order, including folding all her clothes neatly and placing them on the table next to each other but not touching. If they touch each other she unfolds them all and starts again.

Area of perfectionism: organisation/order. Mia appears to only have one main area of perfectionism, however this appears to affect many aspects of her day.

Possible underlying need: sensory. Mia's whole world appears to centre around her feeling as though things are in 'their right place'. She seems to gain a tremendous sense of control from this. It may be that she finds her environment overwhelming and is reassured through the visual and repetitive act of checking and organising. Mia would benefit from an exploration of her sensory needs and developing a range of ways to feel calm in her surroundings. Some children like Mia benefit from a 'sensory diet' throughout the day, the use of visual and concrete learning and communication supports, and 'social stories' about what to do with their feelings.

Case study 4: Harrison

Harrison is a teenage boy who is described by his teachers as, at best, 'disaffected' and 'disengaged', and at worst, 'defiant' and 'aggressive'. Harrison has always struggled with his learning and found school hard. He is frequently in trouble with school staff for behaving in disruptive ways. Appearing 'cool' and self-sufficient is very important to Harrison. He comes from a very challenging background and has learned to fend for himself. Other people are not to be trusted so he would never consider asking for or receiving help. He does not consider himself 'clever' in the traditional sense but is driven to making a success of his life, not that he would share this with any of the school staff who he believes are beneath him in terms of life experience and understanding the 'real world'. He does not believe anyone at school cares about him yet sometimes behaves in ways that make school staff want to nurture him. The majority of the time, however, his behaviour provokes them to feel very angry towards him and want him out of the school.

Being very streetwise and confrontational towards authority has helped Harrison feel powerful and in control. Harrison spends long periods of time on his appearance, making sure he is wearing the most current labels and has the trendiest haircut, even if these do not comply with school rules. Harrison becomes very threatening if he is challenged to change into the correct school uniform. He has also been known to physically assault other students who have got his clothes dirty or ruffled his hair. School staff are suspicious that Harrison is dealing drugs to make money to buy his designer clothes and shoes. His parents are separated and do not come in for school meetings, so teachers are finding it hard to move things forward for Harrison. It is likely he will be permanently excluded.

Areas of perfectionism: appearance/dress, relationships. Harrison appears to have two very linked areas of his life affected by perfectionism and these have served a valuable function in reducing his sense of vulnerability in the world.

Possible underlying need: emotional security. Harrison appears to need a nurturing approach that helps him learn that he is worthy of care, that other people can be trusted to be kind and consistent with him and that the world is largely a predictable and safe place to be. His perfectionism will be very difficult to challenge, as it appears to be serving a very primal need for him: survival. The path for Harrison if he does not get support to challenge his attitudes and beliefs is a very depressing one, likely to result in the criminal justice system.

It is important to reiterate that there is not *one kind* of student high in perfectionism. All students are different. The above are examples only and hopefully make some of the theory discussed more tangible. The possible underlying needs are just areas for further consideration; it may be that other areas require intervention once a young person's situation is explored in more depth.

Perhaps you are already beginning to consider the 'dangers' of perfectionism for the above students. The next chapter talks about the risks associated with perfectionism.

Endnotes

1   Starley (2018)

2   Shafran, Cooper and Fairburn (2002, p.778)

3   e.g. Winnicott's (1953) description of 'the good enough mother' now has far-reaching applications to many areas of childcare, including being used to judge the appropriateness of parenting in child protection cases.

4   The six popular perfectionism rating scales:

The Adaptive/Maladaptive Perfectionism Scale for Children (AMPS)

The Almost Perfect Scale – Revised (APS-R)

The Child and Adolescent Perfectionism Scale (CAPS)

The Frost Multidimensional Perfectionism Scale (FMPS)

The Perfectionism Cognitions Inventory (PCI)

The Perfectionistic Self-Presentation Scale – Junior (PSPS-J).

5   Parental expectations; FMPS question 1 and CAPS question 8.

6   Parental criticism; FMPS questions 3 and 5.

7   Organisation; FMPS questions 2 and 7.

8   Stoeber and Damian's (2014) Clinical Perfectionism Questionnaire (CPQ), question 4.

9   Hewitt and Flett's (2004) Multidimensional Perfectionism Scale, question 5.

10 Gaultiere's (2000/2012) Self-Assessment Perfectionism Screening Test, question 7.

11 Crowne and Marlowe (1960)

12 Adelson and Wilson (2009)

13 **Projection:** this is when a person, unable to manage strong feelings, finds ways of making other people feel these things for them so they don't have to experience the pain. An example would be a person who constantly feels 'not good enough' and continually finds fault in others, leading to those around them not feeling good enough themselves. This temporarily helps the person avoid feeling this for themselves as the attention is on someone else. Teachers and parents of young people with mental health difficulties are often left feeling helpless, confused and out of control. These are usually the feelings of the young person being 'projected' into the adult. This is useful information for the adult to notice in themselves. *Ask yourself: is this my feeling or theirs?*

Transference: this is when a person directs feelings towards someone in their current life that are actually intended for someone else from their early life, usually a primary caregiver. An example would be a student feeling a strong need to please their teacher and seek their approval, or a student getting into a 'power-struggle' with a teacher as they do not appear to feel comfortable with the adult being in control. Teachers can often feel puzzled by the strength of feeling directed towards them. It is usually nothing personal that they are doing wrong, but rather something about their status, authority or even gender that has unconsciously reminded the young person of experiences with their caregivers early in life. Again, this is useful information to notice. *Ask yourself: what exactly is the young person feeling towards me and could this actually be their feelings for someone else?*

Counter-transference: this is when the adult experiences feelings towards the young person that may seem out of character; the young person has behaved in a way to prompt the adult to react to them as though they were the person intended above. An example would be a teacher feeling a strong need to comfort and reassure a student, or conversely to avoid and reject a student. They may be 'playing out' the pattern from the young person's early experiences. This is very helpful information to notice and, as with the above, will give powerful information about what the young person is likely to be feeling. *Ask yourself: how am I feeling about the young person and what does this mean the young person needs?* An important thing to remember is that when young people appear to deserve or want our attention least, is when they actually *need* it the most. How we go about giving it to them in a helpful way is discussed in Chapter 7.

14 e.g. Neumeister (2003, 2004)

15 e.g. Neumeister and Finch (2006); Besharat, Azizi and Poursharifi (2011)

16 e.g. Cattell and Mead (2008); Hollender (1978)

17 Pembroke (2012)

18 Weisinger and Lobsenz (1981, p.281)

19 Låftman, Almquist and Östberg (2013)

20 Dahl (2014)

21 Crowne and Marlow (1960)

22 Nolan (2014)

23 Natcharian (2010)

24 e.g. Jaradat (2013)

25 e.g. Rice and colleagues (2007); Thorpe and Nettelbeck (2014)

26 Coren and Lethar (2014); Lyman and Luthar (2014)

27 Greenspon (2000)

28 e.g. van Hanswijck de Jonge and Waller (2003)

29 DiBartolo et al. (2004); DiBartolo, Yen and Frost (2008)

30 Chan (2007)

31 Zhang and Cai (2012)

32 Achtziger and Bayer (2013)

33 Klibert et al. (2014)

34 Nounopoulos, Ashby and Gilman (2006); Stornelli, Flett and Hewitt (2009)

35 Arrazzini and De George-Walker (2014)

36 Dweck (2006)

37 McVey et al. (2004)

38 Chan (2012)

39 DiPrima et al. (2011); Morris and Lomax (2014)

40 Dweck (2006)

41 Damian et al. (2014)

42 Deci and Ryan (2002)

43 Rotter (1954)

44 Maslow (1970)

45 Freud (1937)

46 Flett et al. (2012); Gnilka, Ashby and Noble (2012)

47 Lindberg and Distad (1985)

Chapter 2

Risks of Perfectionism

'Perfectionism: a wolf in sheep's clothing.'

Perfectionism may not appear to be a bad thing. It may, for some, seem harmless, humorous or even helpful.

The important thing to keep in mind is that perfectionism is *neither good nor bad*. It would be too simplistic a view to consider it in these terms. But many of us do; it is a quick and easy way to understand the world. *It is human nature.*

Good for me, or bad for me?

Good for my children, or bad for them?

It is a childlike logic we apply to help streamline our busy lives. We use this way of categorising particularly when we are stressed, to try to make things simpler for ourselves.

Balancing out both sides of an argument and considering the 'middle ground' takes time, effort and flexibility and these are generally dismissed in favour of 'getting the job done'. When it comes to perfectionism this is especially important: reasoning, reflection and rational thought are often absent and a stress-response is more likely to be present. 'System 1' thinking prevails. The world is black-or-white. Do, do do... Don't stop to think and definitely don't stop to feel.

We have already discussed the possible function of perfection-ism as a coping skill in Chapter 1. By the end of this book you will hopefully feel somewhat convinced that life is more complex than things simply being split into either 'all good' or 'all bad'. You will also have ideas about how to help young people take the time to find 'the middle ground'. The ways in which this complexity applies to perfectionism will be explored more in the next chapter.

So why should we be concerned?

Despite this complexity, it cannot be ignored that there have been many research studies[1] suggesting a damaging impact of perfectionism and linking it with diagnosable conditions. For example, Shafran and Mansell (2001) conducted a review of the research and treatment for perfectionism and found that not only is perfectionism highly correlated with 'a broad range of psychopathology' (p.879), but that it is also 'notoriously difficult to treat in adults' (p.900). Early intervention therefore appears necessary.

Perfectionism studies are largely correlational in nature, meaning there can be no 'proof' that perfectionism is the absolute cause of negative outcomes, therefore some caution must be exercised when making links. Nevertheless the evidence points strongly to a link between high levels of perfectionism and a range of detrimental experiences (e.g. aggression, underachievement, mental health problems, poorer life outcomes and suicide), and rather than dismiss this repeated connection as coincidental it is appropriate to make some assumptions about the likely risks of perfectionism. The opposite, ignoring any possible links, feels negligent. The 'middle ground', accepting there may be risks but focusing less on 'pathologising' individuals and instead on helping move towards healthier ways of functioning, is the path taken by this book.

The suggested 'risks' of perfectionism are outlined below.

The risks

There have been considerable risks identified with high levels of perfectionism for many aspects of a person's life; their education, relationships, health and overall self-care and independence. *Please note that the chapter concludes with a candid discussion of death; the concerning link with perfectionism that cannot be ignored.* These risks include:

- feelings of failure, guilt and shame
- the problematic expression of anger
- defensiveness, hypersensitivity to criticism and proneness to social anxiety
- stress and distress
- exhaustion
- headaches
- intrusive mental imagery
- sleep problems, particularly insomnia (perhaps due to high stress levels and low level of balanced life activities)
- low self-esteem
- a passive coping approach
- weaknesses in social functioning and leadership skills
- social isolation
- problematic use of internet communicative services
- school refusal, 'self-handicapping', performance-avoidance and underachievement
- procrastination
- lower efficiency and therefore lower performance
- academic burnout.[2]

These issues may be evident in students during their school years, or they may not actually emerge until the young person leaves school. There are considerable rates of mental health difficulties in Higher Education, perhaps indicative of students who have 'made it through' secondary level education and found that their coping mechanisms no longer work outside the school environment. However, rates of mental health difficulties in school-age children are also increasing, so young people may also be at risk of the above difficulties unless we intervene early.

Links with diagnosable 'conditions'

Perfectionism has links with a range of diagnosed conditions, some of which may come as a surprise. Here is a brief summary:

Anxiety, particularly social anxiety

There are often 'perfectionist' thoughts present in anxiety conditions (e.g. 'I must get this finished'; 'I need to get this perfect'; 'I can't make a mistake') which trigger feelings of anxiety, resulting in a vicious cycle of perfectionist behaviours attempting to alleviate the anxiety. Social anxiety in particular is fuelled by thoughts that others demand perfection from you and that you must 'perform' in certain ways to get approval. Anxiety, maintained over long periods, can lead to depression.[3]

Attachment insecurity

Perfectionist thoughts (e.g. 'I have to do this all by myself'; 'It is not okay to show weakness') can lead to unhealthy and damaging relationships, including with oneself. Perfectionism has particularly strong links with an 'avoidant', 'anxious' or 'dismissive' attachment style. This means that the person has learned not to rely on others to get their needs met and that their emotions must be hidden from view.[4]

Attention deficit hyperactivity disorder (ADHD)

Perfectionism and ADHD may appear to be opposites; one suggesting a high level of organisation and focus and the other a lack of this. However, 'perfectionist' thoughts (e.g. 'This has to happen a certain way') in people diagnosed with ADHD can trigger feelings of anger, resulting in outbursts and stress. Perfectionism can also be seen through procrastination, ineffective time management and abandoned projects due to impossibly high standards and impairments in planning ahead and monitoring their own behaviour. Trying to get things perfect and perseverating on tasks can also be a learned response to having been over-corrected for making careless mistakes and not paying enough attention; a frequent hallmark of the child with ADHD.[5]

Autism spectrum condition

Perfectionism is very closely linked with autism. 'Perfectionist' thoughts (e.g. 'I need this to be exactly so'; 'I have to get this just right') can trigger feelings of distress, resulting in the build-up of tension and 'meltdowns'. 'All-or-nothing' thinking, attention to detail, and a tendency to get 'stuck' and perseverate characterise both autism and perfectionism. Young people on the autistic spectrum also have the social difficulties which make it more likely they will believe others expect perfection from them, and the communication difficulties that make asking for help much more challenging.[6]

Bipolar mood disorder

Self-critical perfectionist thoughts (e.g. 'I am useless'; 'I must be the greatest') are associated with the development of bipolar mood disorder symptoms, particularly where there is also anxiety present. Self-compassion is considered a helpful 'tool' to combat these and relieve the symptoms of bipolar disorder.[7]

Body dysmorphia

There are often 'perfectionist' thoughts relating to how a person feels they should look (e.g. 'I must have a thigh gap'; 'I have to be perfectly toned') leading to compulsive behaviours to attain this ideal, including over-exercising, hours spent on beauty regimes and even cosmetic surgery. The constant seeking of slimmer, harder, better, faster, stronger, etc. has strong perfectionist overtones; there will never be 'good enough' in terms of how a person feels they look: their body image is distorted and their 'ideal appearance' unattainable. This drive for the 'perfect body' can result in serious health problems. Body dysmorphia has been associated with the media and culture of our times, for both men and women, and is closely linked with eating disorders and 'perfectionist' thinking.[8]

Depression

Perfectionist thoughts (e.g. 'I am not good enough'; 'Other people think I'm a failure') can trigger feelings of low mood and a sense of worthlessness, leading to depressed behaviours such as isolation, changes in diet and reduction in hobbies. Aspects of perfectionism that make depression particularly likely are the high levels of shame and self-doubt, frequent comparisons with others, lack of support, fear of rejection or disapproval, and keeping fears and mistakes hidden. At worst, depression is linked with suicide.[9]

Eating disorders

Perfectionist thoughts (e.g. 'I cannot cope with feeling this way'; 'I need to be in control'; 'I am not thin enough') can trigger unhealthy eating behaviours. There is a particularly strong link between perfectionist thinking and eating disorders in young females. Eating disorders have the highest mortality rate of any mental illness.[10]

Obsessive-compulsive disorder

There is a strong link between perfectionism and obsessive-compulsive disorder. Perfectionist thoughts (e.g. 'I have to do this'; 'This needs to be done') can trigger compulsive behaviours, which can trap the individual into an unhealthy loop of thoughts and behaviours attempting to manage feelings of anxiety. The anxiety is often about making a mistake or not doing something 'the right way', which could result, in the person's mind, in something catastrophic taking place.[11]

Self-harm

Persistent perfectionist thoughts (e.g. 'I have to get this done'; 'I can't show weakness') can greatly raise stress levels and inhibit emotional expression, leading to a build-up in emotions and a need for release which some young people achieve through self-harm. Other young people may communicate their inner turmoil, conflict and distress ('I have to be the best/I am not good enough') through self-harm, as they do not yet have the words or 'safe place' to express this. Self-harm may start in a small and reasonably 'controlled' way but can escalate in severity, requiring medical attention or even leading to suicide (accidental or deliberate).[12]

Suicidal ideation and suicide

A young person believing themselves to consistently be 'not good enough' but, feeling the need to achieve and be seen as coping, may eventually 'burnout' with this chronic level of stress and decide that the only way to cope with the turmoil is to take their own lives. This may begin as a fantasy but become a reality.[13]

The real risk of death

This section has not been written lightly. Having worked in psychiatric crisis services and as an educational psychologist responding to 'critical incidents' in schools, I am acutely aware of the gravity of such a topic and its potentially triggering nature for many readers.

Please be mindful of your own self-care and take time to look after your own needs. Read on only when feeling able to do so.

There is a list of support agencies you can contact if required in Appendix B.

Fortunately, suicides in children are very rare, but predicting them is difficult. This section concludes with some possible warning signs for suicide in young people, with some guidance on what to do if you identify risks in young people. This aims to help raise your confidence to approach rather than shy away from this considerable topic.

Perfectionism has links with suicide that cannot be ignored.

UK researchers Bell and colleagues (2010) describe the impact of perfectionism on suicidality as 'particularly intense among academically high-achieving and gifted young people', who have a tendency to find even exceptional achievements 'emotionally exhausting, rather than gratifying'.[14]

The risk of suicide is likely to be greater in students high in perfectionism due to the following 'toxic trio' of factors:

Almost constant high level of stress due to self-imposed pressures and expectations

These young people's stress hormones are likely to be higher due to putting themselves under constant pressure and therefore anxiety to perform. Increased stress chemicals mean their problem-solving skills and overall coping capacity are greatly reduced.

- It is known that increased and persistent stress is a risk factor for suicide.

Unlikely to seek help or support due to perceived sense of failure in doing so

Students high in perfectionism are very unlikely to seek help; it can be perceived by them as an intolerable weakness to even think about needing help, or they may not even be aware they could benefit from support as feel they 'should' be coping: their expectations for what is expected and reasonable to tolerate and what is not is likely to be somewhat skewed. They are often described as 'hiding behind a façade', which means that any difficulties are hard to detect by others. Their social lives may be restricted or what social support they have may not know the 'real them' in terms of their thoughts and feelings.

- It is known that lacking quality social support is a risk factor for suicide.

Likely to thoroughly prepare and therefore complete an effective suicide plan

Because they tend to have a high need for control, detail and precision and tend to give unrivalled focused attention to what they decide to do, their suicide plans are likely to be thorough and very well thought out.

- It is known that a clear suicide plan is a major risk factor for completed suicide.

Perfectionism is a serious matter.

We need to be more aware of our boys who are struggling with perfectionist thoughts.

The link between boys and perfectionism is not well-known in either social or research culture. The general stereotype for someone high in perfectionism tends to be female, and the majority of research has studied women. However, it is believed that a lot of young male suicides in particular may result from a perfectionistic need to preserve an image of flawless competency.[15] In their 2008 study, Adams and Govender found a strong link between 'traditional masculine ideology' and perfectionism in adolescent boys.

Fortunately, over the past decade there has been an increase in research into the link between perfectionism and males, highlighting concerns which we should take seriously.[16] There is still a long way to go, as the majority of these studies focus on young men and centre around body image, eating disorders and athletic behaviour, rather than boys in education with perfectionism related to their studies or social world. This is a deeply worrying omission.

Separate from the issue of suicide but related to the risk of death is the fact that eating disorders have the highest mortality rate of all mental health difficulties due to the physical health complications that come from food restricting, overeating, purging or over-exercising. Also relevant here is the knowledge that chronic stress is linked with a variety of physical health problems that could result in premature death: heart disease, stroke, cancer, lung ailments, accidents and cirrhosis of the liver.

The risk may be low, but the risk is there. And the impact can be catastrophic.

Warning signs for suicide

There is no tool that can accurately predict suicide. A review of suicide risk assessment tools in 2018 by Carter and colleagues suggested that there is imminent need for a clinically appropriate, reliable and valid tool that assesses immediate risk of self-harm and suicide in paediatric settings. There is a range of tools currently available which may be 'good enough' in the meantime. In many ways, we as adults in the young person's life are the best risk assessment tool available.

Examples of online risk assessments free to download include:

- 'Tool for Assessment of Suicide Risk: Adolescent Version Modified (TASR-Am)'[17]

- 'Davies's structured interview for assessing adolescents in crisis'.[18]

In addition, many countries have their own dedicated websites for suicide prevention that offer a range of helpful resources including warning signs, as shown in Table 2.1.

Table 2.1: Suicide prevention support around the world

Region	Suicide Prevention Support	Website
Australia	Suicide Prevention Australia	www.suicidepreventionaust.org
Canada	Canadian Association for Suicide Prevention	www.suicideprevention.ca
International	International Association for Suicide Prevention	www.iasp.info
Ireland	Suicide Prevention Ireland	www.suicideprevention.ie
New Zealand	LifeMatters Suicide Prevention Trust NZ	www.lifematters.org.nz
UK	'Mental Health Toolkit' from the Royal College of General Practitioners Papyrus – Prevention of Young Suicide 'Understanding and responding to children and young people at risk of self-harm and suicide: A guide for practitioners in Cambridgeshire'	www.rcgp.org.uk/clinical-and-research/resources/toolkits/mental-health-toolkit.aspx www.papyrus-uk.org (Type this title into an internet search engine to retrieve the pdf file.)
USA	American Foundation for Suicide Prevention	www.afsp.org

The 'warning signs' in Table 2.2 have been amalgamated from the sources in Table 2.1.

Table 2.2: Warning signs for suicide risk

Warning signs for suicide risk	Comments
Family history of suicide	This makes suicide a more 'real' possibility in the young person's mind.
Psychiatric illness	A diagnosed mental health condition makes the young person more vulnerable.
Substance abuse	This can make a young person more reckless and impulsive. Substance use in the past 24 hours particularly raises the risk.

cont.

Warning signs for suicide risk	Comments
Self-harm	Particularly where this is increasing in severity and relating to 'riskier' behaviours such as small overdoses, which may build up over time.
Poor social supports or problematic environment	The young person may be trying to cope with too much alone and/or isolating themselves.
Depressive symptoms	Including lack of pleasure, changes in eating/ sleeping/activities, anger/impulsivity, increased crying or reduced emotional expression and current problems seeming unsolvable, with the young person feeling hopeless and helpless.
Psychotic symptoms including command hallucinations	I.e. telling them to kill themselves or someone else.
Increased 'acting out' and impulsive behaviour	They may show an increase in 'risky' behaviours, perhaps relating to sexual activity, having more accidents than usual or giving away their possessions.
Suicidal ideation	They have thoughts about suicide and may do so regularly. They may talk about death and dying.
Suicide plan	They have a plan for what they could do to end their life. They have considered how, when and where.
Access to lethal means	e.g. ways in which their suicide attempt could be 'successful', e.g. 'weapons', medication, places of height.
Suicide attempt	Previous attempts make it much more likely a future attempt will take place.

A young person can be considered higher in risk where they have multiple risk factors.

What to do if you are concerned a young person is at risk of suicide

Again, there is a range of guidance available and there is not the scope within this book to cover this area in depth. However, it would be remiss of me not to include the following brief tips about what to do if you are concerned that a young person may be suicidal:

✓ Immediately put in place a SAFETY PLAN including actions for the young person, family and school staff:

  – **young person:**

    * let someone know (in whatever way feels comfortable; this may be using words, showing an image, writing a note or behaving in an agreed way)

    * stay in public areas

    * focus on a distraction task

    * use 'safe pain' techniques

    * talk to a friend.

  – **family:**

    * remove access to lethal means

    * agree frequency of 'checks'

    * keep room door open

    * spend time with the young person engaging in distraction

    * time to talk or listen

    * plan activities

    * have emergency contact details and a clear plan of action for if you cannot keep the young person safe (e.g. call emergency services or present with young person at Hospital Accident and Emergency Department)

    * consider seeking further support from Child/Adolescent Mental Health Services.

- **school staff**:

  * provide a safe space in school

  * provide a named adult to talk to

  * encourage the young person to engage in lessons and activities

  * review their timetable as appropriate

  * provide access to counselling or a school nurse

  * address the underlying issues

  * build confidence and self-esteem through positive activity and responsibility

  * consider seeking further support from Child/Adolescent Mental Health Services.

✓ Review the **SAFETY PLAN** at regular intervals to assess for changes in risk for the young person. Include the young person where possible but remain vigilant; signs of apparent 'improvement' in mood can be a warning sign a young person has resolved to take their own life and have planned how they will do so.

✓ **Look after yourself.** Consider the airplane analogy: we must put on our own oxygen masks before helping others with theirs. Our vital self-care includes trying to make time for:

  - eating well and getting exercise

  - sleep

  - finding opportunities to relax

  - spending time with others who make us feel okay

  - reflecting on what we can and cannot control

  - getting organised

– asking for help

– reminding ourselves about what we love about the young person.

Online guidance about making a safety plan can be found at www.stayingsafe.net/home and looking after yourself at www.papyrus-uk.org/im-worried-about-someone-how-can-i-look-after-myself.

Perfectionism: Root of the problem or symptom of the problem?

Perfectionism has been suggested as the 'root' of a range of mental health problems.[19] Certainly, when mental health problems are 'treated' without addressing underlying perfectionism, the outcomes are disappointing.

However, as discussed in Chapter 1, it may be more helpful to think of perfectionism as a **symptom of an underlying need that has not been met**, rather than the problem itself. There is not enough quality evidence to suggest the impact of 'treating' the perfectionism alone, and what does exist somewhat locates the problem inside the young person:

- the existing treatment literature is focused on the individual needing to change themselves, rather than exploring how their environment and influential adults are developing and maintaining unhelpful beliefs and behaviours.

  This is stigmatising, isolating and disempowering.

Considering perfectionism as a symptom of an underlying unmet need also locates a 'problem' within the young person, but instead:

- frames this as an unmet **human need** rather than something sinister, unusual, abnormal or 'wrong' with the young person. It also provides ways in which the environment and adults can change to make things better.

  This is normalising, validating and empowering.

Figure 2.1 shows this idea more clearly.

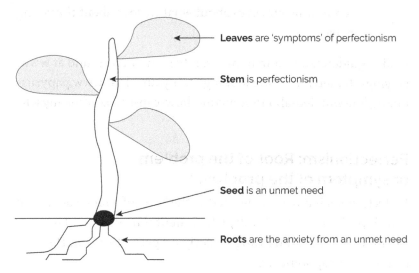

Leaves are 'symptoms' of perfectionism

Stem is perfectionism

Seed is an unmet need

Roots are the anxiety from an unmet need

FIGURE 2.1: MY 'ROOTS AND LEAVES' MODEL OF PERFECTIONISM

The next chapter explores the perceived 'benefits' of perfectionism and considers why it might be so hard for some people to change.

Endnotes

1 Examples of studies suggesting a damaging impact of perfectionism and/or link with diagnosable conditions:

Dour and Theran (2011)

Haring, Hewitt and Flett (2003)

Hewitt and Flett (1991)

McWhinnie and colleagues (2009)

O'Connor, Rasmussen and Hawton (2010)

Shih (2012)

2 Feelings of failure, guilt and shame (Hewitt and Flett 1991)

The problematic expression of anger (Hewitt et al. 2002; Öngen 2009)

Defensiveness, hypersensitivity to criticism and proneness for social anxiety (Flett, Coulter and Hewitt 2012; Roxborough et al. 2012)

Stress and distress (Damian et al. 2014)

Exhaustion (Bell et al. 2010)

Headaches (Kowal and Pritchard 1990)

Intrusive mental imagery (Lee et al. 2011)

Sleep problems, particularly insomnia (perhaps due to high stress levels and low level of balanced life activities; Azevedo et al. 2010)

Low self-esteem (Rice and Preusser 2002)

A passive coping approach (Chan 2007)

Weaknesses in social functioning and leadership skills (Chan 2007)

Social isolation (Flett, Coulter and Hewitt 2012)

Problematic use of internet communicative services (Casale et al. 2014)

School refusal, 'self-handicapping', performance-avoidance and underachievement (Atkinson et al. 1989; Kearns, Forbes and Gardiner 2007; Greenspon 2000; Shaunessy 2011; Damian et al. 2014)

Procrastination (Burnam et al. 2014)

Lower efficiency and therefore lower performance (Stoeber and Eysenck 2008)

Academic burnout (Saviz and Naeini 2014)

3   e.g. Blankstein and Lumley (2015); March *et al.* (1997)

4   e.g. Besharat, Azizi and Poursharifi (2011); Enns, Cox and Clara (2002); Neumeister and Finch (2006); Stoeber (1998)

5   e.g. Conners *et al.* (1998)

6   e.g. Greenaway and Howlin (2010); Fung (2009)

7   e.g. Corry *et al.* (2013); Fletcher *et al.* (2019)

8   e.g. Buhlmann, Etcoff and Wilhelm (2008)

9   e.g. Affrunti and Woodruff-Borden (2014)

10 e.g. Boone, Claes and Luyten (2014); Franko *et al.* (2004); Leung, Wang and Tang (2004)

11 e.g. Park *et al.* (2015)

12 e.g. O'Connor, Rasmussen and Hawton (2010)

13 e.g. Flett (2014); Nauert (2014); Beevers and Miller (2004); Dahl (2014); Donaldson, Spirito and Farnett (2000)

14 Bell *et al.* (2010, p.253 and p.257)

15 Törnblom, Werbart and Rydelius (2013)

16 e.g. Rivière and Douilliez (2017); Schwartz and colleagues (2010); Hasse, Prapevessis and Owens (2002); Boone and colleagues (2012)

17 Kutcher and Chehil (2007)

18 Davies (2013)

19 e.g. Shafran, Egan and Wade's (2010) roots and leaves model

Chapter 3

The Illusory Benefits of Perfectionism

'Surely high targets, focus and dedication are good things?'

Few would dispute the above point. High targets, focus and dedication are surely good things in the world of education and life beyond. People frequently make links between perfectionism and these things, and therefore believe that perfectionism is a largely positive thing. I hope that by the end of this chapter you will come to see that these perceived benefits of perfectionism are in fact an illusion.

I firmly stand by the idea that there is no such thing as 'positive' or 'healthy' perfectionism, supporting leading perfectionism researchers Flett, Hewitt and Greenspon in arguing that *all* forms of perfectionism are unhealthy in the long term. Greenspon is confident that 'healthy perfectionism is an oxymoron' and that believing otherwise is potentially dangerous to children's development.[1] But this view is not shared by everyone. Researcher Lippman (2012), in considering the prevalence of 'perfectionist thinking in cases of depression and eating disorders', asked 'Why do some scholars continue to assert that perfectionism can be healthy?'[2]

Why indeed...? Let us explore the idea of 'benefits' of perfectionism more closely, because it is an idea that cannot be ignored, in both research and popular culture. Perhaps you have your own views around this. What is so great about perfectionism?

The attraction

Many people call themselves 'perfectionists' and the term is frequently used to describe some of the highest achievers in the world of academia, sport, entertainment, politics and business, including:

- **Footballing legend, Cristiano Ronaldo**

  - The sales organisation Frontier Performance describe him as 'the poster child for perfectionism' and talk about 'how perfectionism drives Ronaldo' in relation to helping salespeople perform better in their roles (Frontier Performance 2019).

- **Tennis superstar, Serena Williams**

  - Online 'mental training' site *Sports Psychology for Tennis* relates Serena's 'on-court outbursts' to her 'perfectionist attitude' (Cohn 2013) and *Sporting News* (2014) describes her as a perfectionist.

- **Media personality/entrepreneur/socialite, Kim Kardashian and hiphop star/entrepreneur husband Kanye West**

  - PsychCentral (2014) describes both members of this highly driven couple as perfectionists, suggesting this is a motivating factor in their success.

- **Rap stars, Eminem and Dr Dre**

  - *The Independent* (2009) describes Dr Dre as 'a notorious perfectionist' and Edward Hopkins (2018) states 'we all know Eminem is a perfectionist'.

- **American president and businessman, Donald Trump**

  - *The Guardian* (2015) described Trump as a perfectionist in the lead-up to the presidential election.

There appears to be an everyday assumption that perfectionism is linked with success, and that success equates to happiness. Parents and teachers are likely to refer to a child's perfectionism in largely positive terms, ultimately viewing 'perfect' as positive and desirable. However even the word 'perfect' is misleading, being used in different ways:

- 'perfect' in an absolute, literal sense of being as good as it is possible to be, having no fault or defect, or corresponding to an ideal standard, or

- 'perfect' in a more relative, expressive sense, e.g. to express our satisfaction with food in a restaurant (even if it is not literally 'perfect'), or in response to someone saying they will do something for us on a certain day or time (e.g. pick us up from the station at 7pm). In other words, satisfying all requirements at the current time or in the current circumstances.

In perfectionism, the focus on 'perfect' is perhaps related to either or *both* of these meanings: being both flawless and/or pleasing to others. These things are highly motivating for many people, and generally linked with success. An American website, study.com (2019), describes 'Good Careers for Perfectionists', stating that 'perfectionists can perform very well in just about any career' and specifically naming, amongst others, the following roles as being particularly suited to a 'perfectionist': accountant, interpreter, surgeon, editor. These roles clearly have a high need for precision and accuracy, however this is not necessarily what perfectionism is all about.

In the research world, several studies make links between perfectionism and the following desirable outcomes as compared to 'non-perfectionists':

- *higher* life satisfaction[3]

- *lower* depression levels[4]

- *enhanced* performance[5]

- *greater* achievement[6]

- *higher* peer popularity.[7]

Related to this, some of the available perfectionism rating scales highlight an 'adaptive' form of perfectionism which often describes a 'healthy high-achiever'. This suggests there exists a type of perfectionism that helps an individual to function and succeed. Success is frequently associated with happiness, therefore perfectionism is perceived to be beneficial as it will lead to someone being successful and therefore satisfied with their life. *This is an illusion.*

From examining the literature and my own research into this area, there are five common ways in which the illusion that perfectionism is beneficial manifests itself.

They are as follows:

1. Perfectionism leads to good outcomes.

2. Perfectionism protects against undesirable attributes.

3. Perfectionism helps you cope.

4. Perfectionism gives you an identity.

5. Perfectionism is the path of the righteous.

Each of these will now be considered in turn.

1. Perfectionism leads to good outcomes

Example: a person believing that others like them because of the make-up and clothes they wear, and the way they do their hair. This person is therefore likely to spend a great deal of time, money and effort on their appearance if it is important to them that other people like them (and wanting to be liked by others is human nature for most people). However, if they were to do a cognitive-behavioural experiment and actually find out from people what it is they find attractive, they may be surprised to learn it is *who they are* that is likeable, not the way they look. As long as this person believes it is their appearance which is making them likeable to others, and being liked remains important to them, they are probably going to continue with the high-maintenance beauty regime.

In other words, the individual assumes 'good' things are *because of* perfectionism, when actually they are due to something else.

> **This is a widespread and dangerous illusion which traps an individual in perfectionism.**

THE ILLUSION

Perfectionism is *not* what makes someone successful. This is an illusion that is likely to persist because *some* students high in perfectionism may appear to be very successful. It is therefore easy and tempting to link the perfectionism with the success and even believe that perfectionism *causes* people to be successful. Perfectionism is definitely 'a valued attribute in high-achieving populations',[8] perceived by high-achievers and those around them to be a causal factor in their success.

There is a lot of criticism of this widespread misunderstanding about perfectionism, for example:

- The American Academy of Pediatrics argues that there is a distinction to be made between 'healthy high-achievers' and 'perfectionists'.[9]

- American perfectionism researcher Greenspon explains that the features of 'trying to do well' and the 'pursuit of excellence' are confused with, but *not* attributable to, perfectionism.[10]

- UK researchers Shafran, Egan and Wade assert that 'it is very important for us to be clear about the difference between *perfectionism* and the *healthy pursuit of excellence* or *striving for achievement*'.[11]

When this connection between perfectionism and success is examined more closely, the valued elements often identified in 'successful' students include:

- high expectations

- attention to detail

- precision and accuracy

- organisation

- concentration

- drive/ambition

- hard work

- commitment

- reflection on performance

- learning from mistakes.

Let us be clear now that these are **good learning skills**, and they are attributable to something far more desirable than perfectionism; 'optimalism'. This will be explained further in Chapter 4.

THE DANGER

Given someone high in perfectionism would likely identify with the above valued elements, why is it not their perfectionism which is responsible for their success? The confusion and illusion may lie in the *combination* of perfectionism with some of these desirable learning skills, making it seem like perfectionism is the basis of these behaviours.

For example, the above good learning skills are all healthy and desirable, *until* they are combined with perfectionist attributes:

- High expectations and aspirations are helpful *until they are combined with* a low tolerance for failure and mistakes.

- Attention to detail is helpful *until it is combined with* an inability or refusal to see the bigger picture.

- Determination to succeed is helpful *until it is combined with* an inability to relax and unwind.

- Being able to put aside emotion to get a task done is helpful *until it is combined with* not allowing emotions to be felt at all.

- Valuing achievement is helpful *until it is combined with* having no other areas of value or interest to balance this out.

These perfectionist attitudes serve to temporarily amplify the good learner skills but by doing so with such a 'tunnel-vision' approach, they actually stop them being helpful. The short-term gain and long-term risk of burnout becomes more apparent through this lens.

Therefore perfectionism is actually better understood as the 'toxin' that can cause healthy learning behaviours to become less healthy for the individual. Developing balance, flexibility and compassion are important approaches which will be addressed in more detail in Chapter 6. Some students high in perfectionism may be achieving success; however, without their perfectionist attitudes they could be reaching *even greater* heights, not to mention having better emotional wellbeing.

THE TRAP

This confusion is significant when considering motivation to change. Perceived benefits are a barrier to change, despite the presence of adverse consequences, particularly if the perceived benefit is an area of value to the individual.

This was reinforced in my research (see Appendix A), in which young people, staff and parents associated perfectionism with positive behaviours such as striving, conscientiousness and neatness and with desirable outcomes such as success and self-confidence. However, they also associated perfectionism with less positive thoughts and feelings, such as stress, paranoia, torment, dread and misery. In spite of these things, the outcomes appeared a more motivating factor such that the less pleasant thoughts and feelings could be overlooked. In other words, 'it doesn't matter how you get there, just get there'. *The only thing that matters is the goal.*

There was also a bias towards believing students high in perfectionism were less likely to make mistakes and that they *are actually perfect*. In other words, there was a perception of these individuals as flawless, as opposed to merely seeking to be flawless. Because mistakes were generally perceived as a bad thing, with associations being made between making mistakes and negative or even disastrous outcomes and the idea that someone was a 'failure', people tended towards the 'ideal' of a student who does not make mistakes. This is despite movements towards a 'growth mindset' culture in which mistakes are viewed as the pathway to deeper learning and progress. Making mistakes is a crucial part of development, yet disastrous for someone high in perfectionism. If we were stop and reflect on this 'ideal' student, we would realise that they are unlikely to be doing any quality learning or building the resiliency skills needed for higher education and/or the 'real world'.

THE CONFLICT

Success is associated with happiness and satisfaction. For the person high in perfectionism, the perfectionism is seen as the way to success. However, this leads to an internal conflict, since perfectionism is also linked to less positive thoughts and feelings such as stress, paranoia, dread and misery. The individual therefore faces a paradox: perfectionism leads to success which will make me happy but perfectionism also makes me miserable. How can a person be high in perfectionism, successful *and* happy?

Perfectionism, success and happiness cannot co-exist.

This realisation can be enough for some people to spark the process of change. We cannot rest with internal conflict and must either try to ignore it or act upon it to change our views. This internal conflict is called 'cognitive dissonance': a mental discomfort caused by holding contradictory beliefs, ideas or values. A resolution of this would be the acceptance that perfectionism is *not* what makes someone successful, and any success gained by someone high in perfectionism is unlikely to make them genuinely happy. Authentic happiness comes from a sense of both pleasure and meaning in one's activities,[12] both of which are likely to be absent or at best, superficial, for the student high in perfectionism. Therefore something else must be driving the success. That 'something else' is described in the next chapter.

For some people, they will resolve their cognitive dissonance by attempting to disregard the conflict and continuing as they were. Familiarity can be more comforting than learning to think about the world in different ways. This is a coping mechanism to manage the discomfort, but it must be sensitively challenged over time and replaced with new ways to tolerate discomfort, as going through life with perfectionism guiding the way risks a whole host of negative outcomes.

SUMMARY

The start of this chapter stated that high targets, focus and dedication are good things. On the whole, they are, and few would dispute that. But when driven by perfectionism and therefore in the absence of balance, they are not. They *may* result in short-term gain, for some people, but are likely to cause long-term pain and actually stifle progress and achievement. When they represent the healthy pursuit of excellence, they are driven by much more positive and stable underlying thoughts and feelings, and therefore are more likely to provide lasting success and all-important emotional wellbeing.

This element has been about people seeking desirable outcomes. The next element takes a different angle, the 'benefit' of perfectionism as preventing a person becoming everything they wish to avoid.

2. Perfectionism protects against undesirable attributes

Example: a person who is very conscious of their weight and body shape believing that the opposite of this is being lazy, overweight and disgusting. This person is likely to go to great lengths to pay close attention to their calorie intake, their exercise levels and the way they look. They may fear that if they stop, even for a moment, caring about their body image, they may suddenly become the fat, ugly 'mess' they most fear. This is a good example of all-or-nothing thinking and catastrophisation: the belief that not maintaining who they think they are will set them on a very 'slippery slope' to becoming their worst nightmare self, a person wanted by no one. An unbearable 'opposite' to who they want to be.

In other words, the individual is staying with perfectionism because becoming 'the opposite' is too unbearable.

This popular and powerful fear traps an individual in perfectionism.

THE 'NON-PERFECTIONIST' STEREOTYPE

A powerful barrier to change, and therefore often considered to be a benefit of perfectionism, is a fear of its perceived 'opposite'. How would you describe the opposite of a perfectionist? The idea of a 'non-perfectionist' for many, based upon popular stereotypes of a 'perfectionist', is likely to include a whole range of 'undesirable' characteristics, such as:

- lazy
- uninterested
- unmotivated, doesn't care
- unfocused
- unsuccessful
- disruptive or rebellious, non-conforming
- careless, makes a lot of mistakes
- takes risks and is impulsive.

Most students, staff and parents would agree these qualities are *not* what they would want for themselves or their young people.

AVOIDANCE

Without awareness of the risks of perfectionism and understanding of its nature, young people, staff and parents generally want themselves and their students to be higher than lower in perfectionism! For many, a perceived benefit of perfectionism is the *avoidance* of becoming one or more of the above 'undesirable' characteristics which are being perceived as the opposite of perfectionism. Perfectionism is, therefore, felt to **protect** them from these unwanted ways of being, and what it might mean about them or what might happen if they were to become those things.

- 'As long as I am striving for perfection, I am avoiding being *that* person' (which would lead to me being rejected).

- 'As long as my student is taking great care and attention over their work, they will not fail' (and I will not be seen as a useless teacher).

- 'As long as my child is behaving beautifully, they will not be seen as "the naughty one"' (and I will not be seen as a bad parent).

This is a false attribution of cause. Individuals are assuming that the perfectionism is keeping them safe from being (and being seen to be) lazy, unsuccessful and disobedient. These things presumably could result in feelings of rejection, disconnection and even abandonment. Therefore, ultimately, they believe the perfectionism protects them from rejection; it gives a sense of acceptance. It is a way to survive. This thinking is 'faulty' because it is not perfectionism that is 'protecting' them from these attributes and deeper fears. In the examples above, it is more likely to be diligence, attentiveness and amenability. This is explored further in the next chapter.

THE CONFLICT

In my research it was apparent that although many would associate 'non-perfectionists' with the above undesirable characteristics, they would also perhaps consider these people to have much more pleasant thoughts and feelings than someone high in perfectionism, such as contentment, peace and relaxation. The idea of someone who is not a perfectionist is presumably someone who is:

- more likely to 'go with the flow'

- has no desire to 'be the best'

- probably less critical of themselves and others

- doesn't seem to mind making mistakes

- confident to take risks

- happy with what they've got and how things are.

So, if this type of person is *less* likely to be successful but *more* likely to be happy, *how can we continue to associate success with happiness?*

This realisation can prompt for people the growth in ideas around what they understand by success and happiness, and how these things link with perfectionism. The 'grey area' becomes greater and perfectionism becomes far less 'black-or-white'. This can be a period of confusion as our brains try to work out what it is we believe and understand. The next chapter provides a resolution to this conflict, along with the hopeful message that success and happiness can both be achievable.

A MORE DESIRABLE OPPOSITE

Part of the problem here is not only in the inaccurate description of a person high in perfectionism (high-achiever, good learning skills), but also the inappropriate qualities attributed to someone low in perfectionism (low-achiever, poor learning skills). Just like someone high in perfectionism, someone low in perfectionism, or not showing perfectionism at all, is much more three-dimensional than this. They are also much more desirable than many would first think from the popular stereotype. The next chapter describes a 'positive opposite' of perfectionism to help challenge this belief that the opposite of a perfectionist is someone we definitely wouldn't want ourselves or our students to be.

SUMMARY

Avoiding a negative outcome would be a helpful benefit of perfectionism, if the negative outcome wasn't also an illusion. These first two elements have challenged the ways in which perfectionism and 'non-perfectionism' are understood, making 'benefits' a redundant concept.

The next element takes a compassionate view about a more likely 'benefit' of perfectionism for some people, regardless of its definition.

3. Perfectionism helps you cope

Example: a person who repeatedly checks that everything is switched off and all the locks of their house are secure before they will leave the house. So far, there has been neither a house fire nor any burglary, so the person's belief that they need to perform multiple checks and their behaviour in doing so has helped them – in their mind – keep their home safe. Why would they change this if they believe it to be working?

Well, perhaps the multiple checking takes up so much time that they are frequently rushing and late for where they are trying to go. They could experience being ridiculed or mocked by friends and family for their 'obsessive' ways. Perhaps the thoughts about having to check and check again, then again, are actually quite stressful and intrusive rather than reassuring and calming. Maybe a person like this has the dual experience:

I need to keep doing what I'm doing **and** I wish I could change/ handle this differently.

In other words, the perfectionist thoughts and behaviours are what have so far kept a person feeling 'safe' and coping with life as best they can.

> **This complex and dependent relationship**
> **traps an individual in perfectionism.**

A NEEDED WAY TO COPE

The main 'benefit' of perfectionism appears to be as a **coping skill**. It represents a way of thinking about oneself, other people and the world that has helped a young person get to where they are today. In terms of 'safety', it has helped them 'fit in' to their family unit, function in their school life and manage the challenges of life so far. It may be that for many individuals it continues to function as a coping mechanism for many of their school years; after all, the school environment generally reinforces the idea of success, minimal mistakes and low emotional expression. It may also 'work' as a coping skill into early adulthood. Seeking perfection is seen as helping the person avoid unpleasant confrontations, uncomfortable emotions and continue to be the person they feel they need to be to get their needs met.

However, perfectionism has limited life span as a coping method, as it cannot withstand some of the more challenging aspects of life. The real world is just too messy and unpredictable for such tight control over one's emotions and behaviours.

> **Until a young person has alternative coping skills at their**
> **disposal, they will cling onto what they are used to using,**
> *even if they know these are having a negative impact.*

Some of the stress experienced by young people high in perfectionism comes from a desire to be different and less stressed, but without the knowledge about how to do this. The greater the stress levels, the more the coping skills are needed, and the familiarity of perfectionist ways of thinking and behaving are reinforced through practice time and again. It is a vicious cycle that is not easily broken by the young person alone.

TIME TO SAY GOODBYE

Take a moment to consider some of the 'big events' that inevitably take place in adult life, over which we have limited control. Also take time to consider the vast range of responsibilities presented to us as adults, of which we have limited experience in our childhood and adolescence. Can you imagine getting through these things and balancing your responsibilities without allowing yourself to feel, without being vulnerable and taking risks to problem-solve and 'survive the storm', and without seeking or at the very least allowing yourself to receive some sort of support?

Instead of demonising perfectionism, I prefer to think of it as a coping method that has served its purpose in keeping the person safe. It has helped them experience some sense of control in a world that can feel overwhelming and hard to understand. It is now time to say thank you, and good bye, and to welcome new and healthier ways of coping with life that will give the young person greater access to a rich and fulfilling experience and the skills to cope with whatever challenges life throws at them. This is not an easy goodbye! As with addictions and self-harm, which can also be understood as coping skills people use to attempt to manage distressing or overwhelming feelings, there will need to be a gradual move towards new and better ways of coping. This will require huge amounts of patience, commitment and compassion.

SUMMARY

The idea of perfectionism as a coping skill is the most genuine 'benefit' to be understood. Keeping tight control over one's emotions and behaving in particular ways may have worked brilliantly for helping the young person make the world feel more predictable and therefore helping them feel they can cope. However, given the risks discussed in Chapter 2, it is wise to think about saying goodbye to the perfectionism and welcoming in new ways of coping that are more likely to bring lasting success and happiness. We must of course take great caution in doing this, so that other unhealthy ways of coping are not unintentionally introduced.

The next element explores a 'deeper' version of this, and one which brings its own challenges.

4. Perfectionism gives you an identity

Example: a person who believes perfectionism is a personality trait and something you are either born with or you are not. For their entire childhood so far they have been called a 'perfectionist' by others: their family, friends and school staff. It is a label that has stuck and become an important part of how they see themselves. 'I am a perfectionist.' It becomes an explanation...an excuse...for things they do. It is confusing and somewhat distressing when they hear people talk about perfectionism as being 'unhealthy' or a 'bad' thing, or when it is mocked. Does that mean they are 'unhealthy', 'bad' or 'ridiculous'? In which case, why are people constantly praising the things that make them who they are? 'Who am I supposed to be?' is the tormented voice within.

In other words, 'being a perfectionist' is what gives the individual a sense of self. Without that, who are they?

This needed sense of self traps an individual in perfectionism.

STABILITY

Our identity – the enduring qualities that make us who we are – is something that helps us feel stable through our experiences. It is unshaken by daily events and reinforced or enhanced by challenges and achievements. A person's identity 'anchors' them into their life and helps them make meaningful connections with others: people they 'identify with'. It guides their choices and behaviours in ways that feel predictable to others. It can be seen, amongst other things, through the way they dress, the activities they engage in and the path they take through life. Someone with a stable identity has clear patterns of behaviour and ways of viewing themselves and others. These are helpful things to make the world less stressful.

For some young people with high levels of perfectionism, their identity may be built around the idea of themselves being 'a perfectionist'. This idea, whether positive or negative to them, will provide them with some sense of stability and constancy to return to at times of challenge, including when things around them are changing. In many ways, this appears to be a 'benefit' of perfectionism insofar as it grounds the individual and gives them a sense of control. It also makes them more predictable to others so other people are likely to behave in reliable and consistent ways towards them, again helping them feel in greater control over their experiences.

INSTABILITY

Not having a clear identity can be unsettling, destabilising and create a whole host of emotional and behaviour problems for us. A person with an unstable sense of self, a less enduring identity, is more at risk of mental health problems. Some of the more serious mental health conditions represent a total instability of identity, such as Dissociative Identity Disorder and Borderline (Emotionally Unstable) Personality Disorder.

An individual without a stable sense of who they are may use behaviours to try to present a certain image of themselves to others, in a way that 'compensates for' or tries to mask who they feel they really are. Keeping up such an 'act' may be exhausting and unsustainable, leading to a range of social-emotional problems. Using different behaviours may also be an attempt by the person to 'find' who they are by trying out lots of different personas. This can be unsettling for themselves and others. It is human nature to need a sense of stability, constancy and predictability. A person with an unstable identity is unlikely to display these characteristics, and when they do, they are likely to be unsustainable.

WHAT IS 'NORMAL'?

Periods of identity instability are a normal part of life. Such 'identity crises' are a typical part of human development and expected at different points in the lifespan. Consider the youthful quest for independence and trying out different ways of talking, dressing and behaving in order to 'find oneself'. Consider also the middle-age quest for freedom and fun, seen through changes in activities and lifestyle.

Our identity can also be challenged at different points in our life, as new experiences present themselves to us. Examples include becoming a parent, getting a job, losing a loved one, coming out, having a major accident, achieving something spectacular or failing spectacularly, etc. We naturally go through stages of identity development which involve periods of feeling unsettled as we adjust to our changing persona.

Finally, our identities can also be unsettled by engaging in different forms of psychotherapy which prompt us to consider who we are as we develop greater self-awareness. Having someone comment on or question aspects of yourself or your behaviours can lead to the cognitive dissonance described above. Attempts to resolve the discomfort of this are often what prompt 'breakthroughs' and progress in psychotherapy. Periods of change in our identity can range from distressing to exhilarating, with everything in between. The important thing to remember when considering perfectionism as an identity is that **our identity is open to change throughout our lifespan**. People change, and that is okay.

Summary

We all need an identity, a stable sense of who we are. Without this, life can be more stressful and we can feel out of control. Perfectionism for some young people may be the 'anchor in the storm' that they have clung to in order to feel a greater sense of stability in an otherwise chaotic world. Like coping skills, a person's identity can be shaped and moulded into something healthier and more functional. Just as people take on certain identity 'labels' to help them gain a sense of stability: 'the joker', 'the naughty one', 'the artist', 'the angel', 'the cool kid', 'the stupid one', etc., so too will 'the perfectionist' need some gentle nudges in the right direction to support them to see themselves in a much more balanced and helpful light. This will clearly take time, patience and commitment. However, it is of vital importance; we do not want our young people to gain their identity from perfectionism; this provides them with unachievable ideals, and therefore an identity that cannot be 'lived up to', leaving them lacking an identity or in a state of conflict in which they believe themselves to be 'a perfectionist' but feel unable to achieve perfection.

The next element brings together the above in addressing a unique aspect of some people's experiences, coping skills and identity: their religious views.

5. Perfectionism is the path of the righteous

Example: a person who wholeheartedly believes their religion expects them to behave in certain ways and live up to particular ideals, and there will be serious repercussions if they do not. They hold extreme views about people's behaviours. This person is likely to live their lives in a constant quest to be the person they believe their religion expects them to be, perhaps critical of themselves and others for not reaching the high standards expected of an 'ideal follower' of the faith. This may cause them to behave in ways others find hard to understand or in ways they would not do if they did not hold such rigid religious views. They are unlikely to question their behaviours, as their motivation is something inexplicable through science and unlikely to be understood by those not following the faith.

In other words, something higher and bigger than scientific research is informing the individual's beliefs and behaviours.

This unquestioned faith traps an individual in perfectionism.

THERE IS SUCH A THING AS PERFECT

I was taught a valuable lesson in my research when claiming 'there is no such thing as perfection' in my attempt to move people away from perfectionism. I no longer believe this extreme, as I have had the chance to reflect on the many moments of 'perfection' I have witnessed and experienced in my own life. I now understand that the idea of 'perfection' is subjective and represents individual values and experiences:

- A person can be perfect to another but imperfect to themselves.

- A person can be perfect in their own mind, but far from this to their loved ones.

- An experience can be one person's 'perfect' and another's 'disaster' or 'nightmare'.

However the reason the above idea was challenged by one of my research participants was over his Christian faith and belief that 'God is perfect' and that it was his role as a 'good Christian' to try to live up to this idea of perfection: to be a 'perfect man' through following the footsteps of Jesus Christ. For him, his whole religious foundation was based on his interpretation that a person *can* and *should be* perfect. His life was dedicated to being as perfect as he could be in everything he did, and also encouraging his children to do the same. Therefore religious belief, for some, may suggest that being perfect is expected, good and a duty of faith.

COMPASSIONATE FAITH

Balance, compassion and love may reasonably be considered a greater part of the teachings of major world religions than extremism and criticism, even though the latter receive more media attention. It is therefore fair to assume that religions (and God/gods) do not wish followers to pursue actions which are harmful to themselves, including restricting their potential and 'gifts'. Therefore any calls to 'be perfect' within a religion should explicitly sit within a framework of compassionate love so that *not* being perfect is not a failure and the individual is still loved (by other people, and, by their God/gods).

For the parent described above, I would want him to develop a more nuanced belief, still sitting comfortably within his Christian faith, to take the place of this 'black-or-white thinking':

'I am good enough as I am *and* I can aspire for perfection.'

Likewise for his family: 'I love my children just as they are *and*

I can encourage them to aim high.' Holding both these ideas is a complicated process but ultimately the sign of a flexible and wise mind. It introduces the important notions of balance and compassion, which help to neutralise the potential toxicity of unrelenting high standards. This is explored further in Chapter 6.

AND IT HARM NONE, DO AS YOU WILL

I cannot dispute or otherwise challenge anyone's religious beliefs; these are valued notions that speak deep to one's core and for many are often unshakeable and of vital importance to their sense of identity and way in which they manage life's ups and downs. What I can and will do, however, is challenge any beliefs that result in harm to anyone, including the person themselves.

Aspiring to perfection may not be a problem in and of itself, and may in fact be a highly motivating and driving force behind growth and success. It is instead the thoughts and feelings that are generated when the person fails to meet these high expectations which are the source of distress. What is the belief *alongside* the aspiration that is resulting in a compulsive rather than motivated drive to perfection?

For this individual I suspect it was a related notion that anything less than perfection was simply not good enough. His belief was likely to be:

'I am aiming for perfection and anything less is a failure.'

This belief also translated to his family: 'I expect my children to aim for perfection and anything less is a failure.' The impact of this was sadly seen through his children's deteriorating mental health and school refusal behaviour.

SUMMARY

Perfectionism may reflect particular religious views; however, balance and compassion are elements of many religions yet things that are missing from perfectionism. Therefore a person demonstrating perfectionism in the name of their religion may be missing the 'bigger picture' of their religion's teachings and ones which would help them live a more flexible and satisfying life, while still remaining true to their faith. Perfectionism, in this context, is not a benefit in terms of, for example, allowing a disciple to get closer to God, but neither does this deny God's perfection or the possibility of a 'perfect' life (e.g. in Buddhism). Rather it recognises that aspiring for perfection can be combined with a belief that 'I am good enough as I am.'

'Benefits' or illusions?

I hope that the above five points will have clarified two things for you:

- Any 'positive attributes' associated with perfectionism are not actually unique to perfectionism.

- Any 'positive attributes' of perfectionism are tainted by the toxins of perfectionism.

The next chapter seeks to resolve some of the conflicts raised in what you have read so far, by introducing you to the 'positive opposite' of perfectionism and the target for all our interventions; 'optimalism'.

Endnotes

1 Greenspon (2000, p.197)

2 Lippman (2012, p.3)

3 Wang, Yuen and Slaney (2009)

4 Afshar *et al.* (2011)

5 Lundh (2004); Stoll, Lau and Stoeber (2008)

6 Roedell (1984)

7 Gilman, Adams and Nounopoulos (2011)

8 Bell *et al.* (2010, p.254)

9 American Academy of Pediatrics (2014)

10 Greenspon (2014)

11 Shafran, Egan and Wade (2010, p.14)

12 Ben-Shahar (2008)

Chapter 4

The Positive Opposite to Perfectionism

'Good enough is perfectly okay.'

We have explored perfectionism, its risks and illusory benefits, and now we will address an important aspect of this book: the 'positive opposite' of perfectionism. We know this is needed because, along with the misinformed perceived benefits of perfectionism, there are also common misconceptions about the person who is opposite to someone high in perfectionism.

This person, considered 'low' in perfectionism, for many is considered to be:

- lazy

- someone who does not care

- unlikely to achieve

- probably disruptive and gets in trouble a lot.

This idea is a powerful barrier to change for those high in perfectionism. They worry that if they reduce or even lose their perfectionism, they will become all the things they do not want to be. Key adults in their life – parents/carers and school staff – are also unlikely to want the young people to be these things, so are more likely to reinforce the behaviours they see as opposite – perfectionism.

The opposite of perfectionism is a good thing

To move away from this difficulty with addressing perfectionism when a person might associate it with desired outcomes and fear becoming the opposite, it is helpful to consider a more 'positive' and desirable opposite. This would help people resolve the conflict between success and emotional wellbeing by creating the belief that **both are possible.**

Ben-Shahar (2009), based on his own experiences with perfectionism, introduced the term **'optimalist'** to describe someone with realistic high standards and a more compassionate view of themselves and others.

An optimalist is a person who accepts and makes the best of everything that life has to offer.

Compared with 'perfectionists' who reject everything that deviates from their flawless, faultless ideal vision (and as a result, suffer whenever they do not meet their own unrealistic standards), 'optimalists' accept the existence of failure, painful emotions, success and reality. They measure success and happiness against standards that are actually attainable.

'Optimalists' are considered to have:

- a healthy mentality

- more balanced thought processes

- more diverse activities

- greater emotional wellbeing.

This mirrors a 'growth mindset'; however it perhaps offers a more pleasing use of language for students: 'optimal' rather than 'perfect' feels desirable yet attainable, particularly as those high in perfectionism are likely to be outcome-focused so the idea of 'growth', which feels more 'process-oriented', may not yet be motivating.

Rather than encouraging students to be perfect or perform perfectly, it may be more beneficial for their wellbeing and subsequent achievement that we instead encourage them to be **optimal** and to perform **optimally**. The focus here shifts to doing only what is needed for a favourable result, compassionately taking into account all factors.

The term 'optimalist' as opposed to 'adaptive perfectionist' has a vital difference; it removes any association with the notion of perfectionism, which for many, as explored in Chapter 3, has connotations which may prevent positive change.

What is optimalism?

Optimalism is about balance, flexibility and compassion. The self-worth of a person high in optimalism is a **realistic and fair balance** of all their virtues and shortcomings, spread across all areas of their life:

- school/work

- health

- relationships

- daily living

- community/recreation

- spirituality/purpose.

If we were to imagine a 'pie chart' of these above areas, an example of the difference in focus between someone high in perfectionism and optimalism can be seen clearly in Figure 4.1. In this example, 'school/work' is the area of value; however, any of the other areas could also be disproportionately high.

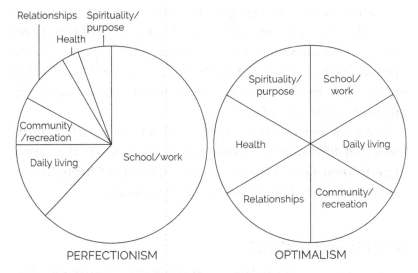

FIGURE 4.1: CONTRASTING PERFECTIONISM AND
OPTIMALISM IN TERMS OF BALANCE OF ACTIVITIES

As we did with perfectionism, let us now visit the thoughts, feelings and behaviours associated instead with optimalism:

Thoughts

- realistic high standards

- failure is used as feedback

- focus on journey *and* the destination

- nuanced, complex thinking

- benefit finder

- forgiving

- open to suggestions

- adaptable, dynamic

- growth mindset.

Feelings

- calm

- contented

- confident

- proud

- successful

- healthy.

Behaviours

- conscientious

- focused

- inquisitive

- risk-taking

- organised

- balanced

- embraces life

- socially connected.

Some people may already have more of these qualities than others, but the important thing is that these are all things that **can be learned**.

We can now consider a different continuum from that described in Chapter 1, which showed the range of possibilities between low and high perfectionism, with the clear message that *no* level of perfectionism is healthy for the individual in the long-run. So where do students go if we want them to be off that continuum altogether? An alternative continuum, shown in Figure 4.2, has perfectionism at one end, but **optimalism** at the other.

Optimalism   Perfectionism

FIGURE 4.2: A DIFFERENT PERFECTIONISM CONTINUUM

This is a continuum on which we *all* reside, not just those showing signs of perfectionism. The opposite end to perfectionism has now become a more desirable place to approach rather than somewhere to avoid. In doing this, we can better motivate students high in perfectionism to move away from their current 'fixed' point. They are no longer 'stuck' where they are and do not have the limited choice of having 'high' or 'low' levels of perfectionism. They do not even have to have any signs of perfectionism! The picture has become less 'black-or-white' and there are options. Importantly, these options can speak directly to the values of the young person, which simply becoming 'less perfectionist' did not offer. They are now being encouraged to become 'more optimalist', to have the chance of being both successful *and* happy in the long term. A motivating and desirable course of action.

Table 4.1 highlights the subtle but important differences between perfectionism and optimalism. At different points along the spectrum the young person would be more or less of these things, rather than all-or-nothing. Our 'ideal student' would be closer towards the optimalism end, demonstrating more of the qualities described in the 'Factors relating to optimalism' column.

Table 4.1: Factors relating to perfectionism and optimalism

Factors relating to perfectionism	Factors relating to optimalism
• Eager to please/approval-seeking	• Self-assured
• Concern pre-task	• Excitement for a challenge
• Doubts during task	• Confidence in ability
• Conscientious and organised	• Conscientious and organised; where appropriate, more flexible and dynamic
• High expectations/standards for self	• Reasonable standards for self, including self-forgiveness
• Concern over mistakes post-task	• Learn from mistakes
• Need for admiration	• Secure in self

• High parental pressure	• Parental support and encouragement
• Perfectionistic self-promotion	• Modest and fair about own strengths and limitations
• Nondisclosure of imperfection	• Able to share difficulties and open to suggestions
• Feels have to do their best all the time	• Feels have to do their best when appropriate
• Feels have to be the best all the time	• Feels doing their best is more important than being the best; values progress over 'winning'
• Perceive others to expect highly of them	• Perceive others have realistic expectations of them

Why do we want our young people to be optimalists?

Just as there is no single 'perfectionist', neither should there be considered one particular 'optimalist'. Therefore, again, the rather clunky but person-centred 'high in optimalism' will be used from this point instead of 'optimalist'.

Optimalism is associated with benefits in education, work, leisure, health and relationships. It also relates to a growth mindset (i.e. the belief that intelligence and other abilities are not fixed but are something we can work towards with effort and learning from our mistakes along the way), which is associated with better emotional wellbeing and more effective learning.

**Optimalism can be considered
'the healthy pursuit of excellence'.**

Students high in optimalism feel more in control of their learning and environment and are therefore more likely to be healthier and happier, which are qualities known to result in better learning and outcomes.

Applying an optimalist rather than perfectionist approach means the young person is more likely to take risks and push themselves out of their comfort zone. That, of course, is the way to make real progress and get the most out of life.

Optimalists are life-long learners with the coping skills to help them face reality, take calculated risks, and get the most from their range of experiences.

Optimalism provides a sense of **balance**. It incorporates desirable behaviours with reasonable attitudes. Valued aspirations with realistic expectations. Success **and** happiness.

A person high in optimalism may be just as likely to succeed as someone high in perfectionism (probably more!), but they are also *more* likely to achieve emotional wellbeing because of *how they go about* succeeding. Figure 4.3 shows this with more clarity.

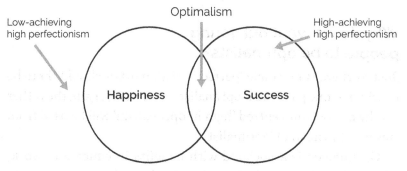

FIGURE 4.3: SUCCESS AND HAPPINESS FOR PERFECTIONISM AND OPTIMALISM

Success and happiness

In his bestselling 2008 book *Happier*, Ben-Shahar explained that happiness can be considered to come from a combination of **pleasure and meaning**:

Pleasure is about deriving **present benefit** from something.

- This is challenging for a person high in perfectionism who is likely to be focused on the end product rather than enjoying the moment.

- Someone high in optimalism will be able to enjoy the process as well, thereby gaining present benefit from their activities as they enjoy engagement and learning for the sake of engagement and learning. Growth!

Meaning is about deriving **future benefit** from something.

- This is more likely than present benefit for a person high in perfectionism, but very short lived and ego-centric. The meaning they attribute to the future benefit is in need of constant updating and reinforcement, and totally tied-up in their self-worth rather than their personal growth or benefit to the wider community.

- Someone high in optimalism will be able to enjoy the future benefit of what they do in terms of adding value to their life, helping them grow and contributing to the bigger picture. This is a much more broad and balanced outlook, leading to a greater sense of fulfilment. Part of this is likely to be the sense of authentic rather than hubristic pride[1] in oneself, i.e. pride experienced through conscientiousness and genuine self-esteem rather than due to narcissism and shame.

Success therefore **can** make a person happy, but only if these two aspects are involved! This is more likely for a person high in optimalism than a person high in perfectionism.

Good stress

In Chapter 1, I mentioned that stress in and of itself is not a bad thing and can actually motivate achievement. It is when stress levels become too *high* that they start to impair performance as our brains can no longer function effectively and we go into survival mode. Equally, when stress levels are too *low*, performance is also affected.

Imagine the following scenarios:

- An event is coming up that you have no interest in, you do not care about the output or about how you perform. What other people think about your performance has no importance for you. The person leading the event is of no interest to you. This event has no bearing on your life or how you see yourself. *Your stress levels for this event are very low and you are unlikely to perform particularly well. You may even avoid the event.*

- An event is coming up that you are totally invested in. It is something of great importance to you and it matters greatly how you perform and how others see you perform. You have the utmost respect and admiration for the person leading the event. Your life and identity is pivotal on your performance in this event. *Your stress levels for this event are very high and this could negatively affect your performance. You may even avoid the event.*

The Yerkes-Dodson Law[2] (curve shown in Figure 4.4) describes the relationship between arousal and performance, highlighting that at low and high levels of arousal (stress), performance (achievement) will be at its lowest. Performance will be at its peak when there is an optimal level of arousal. Therefore some stress is helpful to motivate us to achieve.

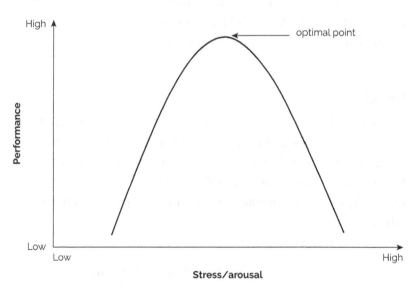

FIGURE 4.4: THE YERKES-DODSON CURVE

A student high in perfectionism is likely to experience one of the above scenarios. This helps to explain why a student high in perfectionism may not reach their potential. Due to their greater level of balanced reasoning and coping skills, a person high in optimalism is more likely to find the middle ground and therefore be better able to perform, no matter how much or little the event has personal significance for them.

Case study examples

There is not yet much research available to further describe optimalism, and it is an idea that is likely completely new to you. Therefore to bring to life the idea of a student high in 'optimalism', here are some case study examples based on students I have known who I would identify as having some 'optimal' qualities.

Do you recognise any young people you know in these descriptions?

Case study 1: Jade

Jade is a primary school girl who is described as 'well-rounded' by her teachers and parents. Jade has a secure group of friends, is confident to try new things and meet new people, and is achieving well in all her lessons. Jade has an active and healthy family life; her parents and siblings all spend time together sharing each others' hobbies and taking time to reflect on their day's experiences. They speak openly about difficulties and any problems they might be having, and talk regularly with the school about strategies that help Jade further improve her literacy and numeracy skills by bringing them 'to life' outside the classroom. Jade also spends time alone in restful, relaxing activities such as reading and doing puzzles. Jade does not yet know what she wants to be when she grows up, and that's okay. Her parents and teachers are happy for her to continue to develop her strengths, practise the things she finds more challenging, and become who she is meant to be over time. Jade won the school end-of-year award for 'Growth Mindset' for demonstrating such fantastic learning qualities. She felt very proud of herself; however, she said that even better than the prize was all the fun she had during the year! She is looking forward to the adventure of next year.

OPTIMALISM IN ACTION

Jade has a supportive and communicative family, a strong social support network, a balanced lifestyle and clearly values the 'journey' of learning. She is likely to approach her schooling and life beyond with resilience and reach her potential in all she does.

Case study 2: Ben

Ben is a teenage boy who is described as 'a good role model' by his teachers. Ben is achieving well in school and is an inspiration to his peers as he has found 'smart' ways of working that do not involve hours of perseverance but still result in quality learning. Ben is modest about this and happy to help others try out his strategies to be more efficient in their work. Ben is a mentor to younger students and speaks openly about mistakes he has made and how he has learnt from them. Ben used to struggle to manage his anger but, with the help of others, has developed self-awareness and a range of strategies over time that now work well for him. Ben aspires to be an architect when he leaves school and knows his strengths in art and imagination will serve him well, and that he needs to further develop his accuracy and maths skills. His teachers are helping him make a plan for how to do this so that he can achieve his goal. Ben is a confident and popular member of the school rugby team and has a healthy diet...as much as any teenager can! Despite having a challenging home life, Ben has a balanced attitude towards life and believes that you can get to where you want to be with the right support and mindset.

OPTIMALISM IN ACTION

Ben has a balanced view of his own strengths and needs and has clearly come a long way in terms of developing his own attitude and skills. He is likely to go on to achieve the things he wants in life and maintain a healthy balance of activities.

Case study 3: Amber

Amber is a teenage girl who is well known in her school and local community for being 'a good egg'. She regularly volunteers to help out at a local soup kitchen and as a companion in a residential care home, organising her time brilliantly to make these things work around her homework. Amber is described as 'an average student' by her teachers; however, they are impressed with how much understated progress she has made during her time at school, despite having specific learning difficulties. Amber has experimented with make-up and designer labels, but does not let these things rule her life; she knows she is liked amongst her peers for her fun-loving and kind nature, and the fact that she always has a listening ear and good advice when needed; that is more substantial than what she looks like and therefore more meaningful to Amber. Amber has a range of people she can turn to when she needs guidance or support, including her best friend, a member of the school support staff and her older brother. She has researched different famous people who have the same learning needs as her so that she has a strong role model for achievement in the face of difficulties. Amber is looking forward to trying out a work experience placement in a nursery to see if working with children is of interest to her.

OPTIMALISM IN ACTION
Amber has a realistic yet positive outlook which allows her to enjoy different areas of her life. She appreciates the value of individual differences and knows her difficulties can be improved with the right support and attitude. Amber is likely to have an interesting path to finding out what she wants to do in her life, and will have fun along the way.

Case study 4: Josh

Josh is a primary school boy who is well liked by his teachers and classmates. Despite not being academically the 'brightest' in the class, Josh has lots of strengths including being a good leader, showing good organisation and planning skills, managing frustrations well and being empathic towards others. Josh did a brilliant job of showing visitors round the school, demonstrating confidence and attentiveness. He is realistic about his own abilities and still prepared to aim high, knowing that 'it is better to try, and fail, than never to try at all'. He is always happy to listen to adults explaining how to do things better and has learnt how to say 'oops, I didn't get that quite right, I'll have another go!' from watching his teacher and parents do this. Josh's parents are very supportive and make sure they reinforce the message that having a go is more important than being the best. Josh is improving his maths and literacy skills by practising for a short amount of time each day. At home, Josh likes playing outdoors with his neighbourhood friends and also learning how to make things out of wood with his granddad.

OPTIMALISM IN ACTION

Josh has a helpful attitude to his education and is happy to take risks, knowing that mistakes are a pathway to greater learning. He has a supportive family and is able to manage his emotions. Josh is likely to continue to improve with practice and find pleasure in a range of life experiences.

A 'richer picture' of optimalism

Stories and metaphor are a helpful way of better understanding something. They allow us to consider things in different ways and make links with things we already know about and understand. What follows is a collection of such stories and metaphors to help bring to life the difference between perfectionism and optimalism and truly promote the desirability of optimalism:

1. The weed and the tree

2. Moths and butterflies

3. The Wizard of Oz

4. Roundabouts and bikes.

These accounts are based on the ideas of Acceptance and Commitment Therapy (ACT) which uses mindfulness and metaphor to develop acceptance of difficulties, and behaviour-change strategies based upon individual areas of value. It aims to be present with what life brings (rather than trying to eliminate difficult feelings) and move closer towards more valued behaviours and 'a life worth living'.

The purpose of our interventions with young people high in perfectionism is to help develop their coping skills so that they take more risks with their learning and development, and ultimately experience more success and happiness in their life. It is not about changing them, it is about **enhancing** them.

Improved coping skills may help to reduce the anxiety underlying perfectionism and remove the need for perfectionism as a coping strategy for life's stresses. Some examples of skills that could be worked on are:

- managing emotions

- expressing self assertively

- developing and maintaining positive relationships

- seeing mistakes as opportunities to learn

- making decisions

- problem-solving

- making and following through a plan.

The following metaphors can provide a starting point for working on some of the above skills, either to aid your own understanding, or to use with the young person themselves to develop their self-awareness and understanding.

Metaphor 1: The Weed and the Tree
1. PERFECTIONISM AND THE WEED

Perfectionism is like a weed.

Weeds can get out of control. They can quickly become unwanted and a nuisance, perhaps even causing damage to other plants or property. Although some can have a superficially pleasant appearance, they generally offer no real value or use to the garden or wildlife. They are strong in the sense of being able to grow just about anywhere, but their survival rates are low as they often have shallow roots and since they are largely unwanted by people, will likely be removed. The flowers or fruits they produce can be bitter, poisonous and cause irritation. Weeds rarely grow particularly strong or tall.

Perfectionism has similarities with this. Behaviours related to perfectionism can very quickly get out of control and become a nuisance to the young person or the people around them. The student's motivations are ego-centric, therefore they offer very little in the way of meaningful engagement or contributions to others. Their drive to succeed (and not fail) is so strong that they will perform their behaviours anywhere, not taking account of their surroundings or considering the most optimal place to perform. Perfectionism can result in bitterness and irritability, leading to a variety of problems, including restricting personal growth.

2. OPTIMALISM AND THE TREE

Optimalism is like a tree.

Trees are strong and enduring, growing slowly but meaningfully after having set down deep and powerful roots which keep them stable throughout storms. They provide leaves, fruits, seeds and shelter for wildlife, including humans. They are both admired and functional, serving a whole variety of purposes, from oxygen replenishment, to aesthetic and therapeutic benefits, to providing us with sap, wood, and paper amongst other products, giving us a place to build our treehouses, attach our hammocks, carve our initials...I'm sure you can add plenty more. Trees have purpose and value. They are grand and dignified, no matter how small, and serve the world around them. Trees effectively adapt throughout the seasons to remain healthy.

Optimalism has similarities with this. Behaviours related to optimalism promote a rich and fulfilling life for the individual. They make the student strong and able to endure a whole host of experiences. Optimalism is about making a positive contribution to the world as well as attaining personal achievement and wellbeing. It is about someone who is adaptable, yet stable and respected by others. Optimalism represents learning at a deep level and flourishing for many years to come. Optimalism as a way of living can be the seed of powerful 'fruits', bringing to life the idea of growth, nourishment, flourishing and health.

Metaphor 2: Moths and Butterflies
1. PERFECTIONISM AND MOTHS

Being high in perfectionism is like being a moth.

The moth is a secretive creature, largely hidden away and avoidant of contact with others, preferring to come out at night. It has dark and depressive connotations and is linked with destruction (e.g. eating through fabrics), being considered a pest by many. It eats in the dark, often things we as humans do not want it to be eating. The moth is perhaps most famously associated with 'seeking the light'. We use the phrase 'like a moth to a flame', meaning compulsively being drawn to something, in spite of its dangers. Moths obsessively chase artificial light sources even when they are causing them harm, or when doing so could risk their lives. Otherwise they prefer dark corners. Typically, moths have muted colours and are traditionally viewed as 'black-and-white' or at least two-tone. Their wings are not perfectly symmetrical, and they have an aversion to lavender, which is why it is a useful plant to use to deter moths from nesting in closets. Even when at rest, moths have their wings open as though ready to move at any point. For many, moths symbolise determination and faith.

Being high in perfectionism is like being a moth. It is like chasing after a (superficial?) goal and ignoring everything else going on around you. It is persisting with the goal even when it is causing you harm: being focused on the prize and disregarding your own wellbeing. It's being drawn towards something that will eventually lead to your own downfall. Perfectionism is being in the darkness and keeping yourself isolated. It is living in 'black-or-white' and hiding in the corner. People high in perfectionism avoid relaxation and can trigger feelings of mistrust, dislike and wariness in others. They may have secretive eating habits and be misunderstood by others. Perfectionism is 'serious'. It does not have space or time for pleasure and enjoyment.

2. OPTIMALISM AND BUTTERFLIES

Being high in optimalism is like being a butterfly.

Butterflies are strongly associated with life. They are colourful and vibrant, and move in a carefree way, fluttering rather than diving in. They are sociable, attracted to a range of colours, scents and objects, and are generally enjoyed and admired by many. They are proudly and confidently out in the open, not hidden away, though they are able to protect themselves when needed. For many, the butterfly represents endurance, change and hope. Their antennas are generally longer than those of a moth. They rest with their wings closed, truly relaxing. They enjoy basking in the sun and taking time to sip nectar from a range of flowers. Their wings are not symmetrical, but no less beautiful.

Being high in optimalism is like being a butterfly. It is being carefree and sociable, able to enjoy the good things in life without being misunderstood or a pest to others. It is coming 'out in the light' and allowing your true colours to shine through; a whole spectrum rather than extremes. Optimalism is about taking care of yourself while also enjoying life and finding the time to truly relax. People high in optimalism are likely to be admired and liked by others as their true beauty shines through and they are unapologetically themselves.

3. TRANSFORMATION AND REBIRTH

Insects are symbolic of rebirth.

Both moths and butterflies can represent change and growth. An individual does not need to remain 'fixed' in their ways, but can instead adapt over time and become 'free': their true selves. Just as the caterpillar transforms into a butterfly or a moth, so too can the young person see themselves as able to change. Instead of viewing themselves as a 'fixed' moth or butterfly (i.e. at the end of their journey), they can take a step back and consider themselves to be at the start of their journey. Will they break free from their cocoon as a moth, or a butterfly? Which 'butterfly' behaviours most appeal to them? What help might they need to become 'more butterfly' and 'less moth'? Can they be a combination of the two? Which 'moth' behaviours would they like to keep and why?

Metaphor 3: The Wizard of Oz
1. Perfectionism and Kansas

Perfectionism is living in a black-and-white world.

Just like Dorothy's life at the beginning of the film, *The Wizard of Oz*, perfectionism is like living in a black-and-white world in which a longing for something more, something better and different, is ever-present. Experiences are frightening, anxiety provoking or just plain boring. Discontent reigns and there is no real pleasure, even from what should be our closest relationships. There is a lack of appreciation for what you have and a lack of awareness of the strengths within. Feeling lost, confused and threatened are the dominant sensations. Perfectionism is serious. There is no place for creativity and adventure. Perfectionism keeps us trapped. We are our own barriers.

2. Optimalism and Oz

Optimalism is living in glorious technicolour!

Just as Dorothy's greyscale view changes when she enters Oz, so too does optimalism change your view of the world. Life is no longer as simplistic or dull as simply 'black-and-white'. There is a multicolour spectrum of experience, with every shade imaginable. A whole range of feelings are present and allowed to flow, as well as accepting and supporting these feelings in others. Challenges suddenly seem surmountable with the guidance of someone more expert, and the support of friends. Plans change, problems can be solved and mistakes learned from. Just as Dorothy 'pulls back the curtain' to reveal the reality of the 'Wizard', so too can optimalism allow us to view and accept the realities of the world, with all its suffering as well as joys. Just as Dorothy defeats the Wicked Witch of the West using courage and intuition, so too can optimalism help us face our fears and overcome them. Optimalism, as with Dorothy's story, allows us to appreciate our strengths within and how far we have come in our journeys, as well as celebrating the strengths of others and supporting them when needed. It helps us recognise that anything is possible by tapping into our hidden strengths and using our social support. It shows us that things are not simply 'black-and-white'. Optimalism frees and empowers us. We are our own Wizard.

3. A BALANCE

We can't be 'on' all the time.

A multicolour explosion can be an overwhelming place to be. Experiencing lots of emotions and social interactions can be exhausting, and we cannot possibly face our fears and challenges every waking moment. Just like Dorothy returns to Kansas at the end of the film, to 'black-and-white', so too can our young people feel reassured that they can make use of comforting experiences that help them feel calm and rested. No one is expecting them to change, and certainly not to change overnight. Boring is sometimes exactly what we need! The skill lies in self-awareness, recognising when we need some 'downtime' and noticing if this is becoming too much or interfering with our progress.

Metaphor 4: Roundabouts and bikes
1. PERFECTIONISM AND ROUNDABOUTS

Being high in perfectionism is like riding a roundabout.

On a roundabout there may be an initial 'rush' and a feeling like you're on the move, but in the end you realise you are just going round and round and the fun of the rush wears off. You might even feel a little sick. The faster you go, the dizzier you get and you will want to get off...though getting off gets harder.

When you are high in perfectionism, you may also experience a 'rush' as you put your efforts into doing or being something perfectly. However, you will soon realise that this is not possible and stress will set in. The more you try to seek perfection, the more stressed you will get. Instead of learning what you could do differently next time, you repeat your familiar ways of behaving and hence go 'round and round' with your belief that you can (and must) achieve perfection, and your behaviours to try and get there. You will always be going round and round without ever getting anywhere.

Just like a roundabout remains rooted to the spot but spinning, so too does someone high in perfectionism. They don't truly learn and move on, instead remaining in a state of stress, and likely to get a headache! It becomes hard to focus on anything else other than trying to keep your balance and wondering how and when you can get off...maybe with a sense of panic that you never will.

2. OPTIMALISM AND BIKES

Being high in optimalism is like riding a bike.

At first you don't even know bikes exist. You are stuck playing in the playground with the other little kids. It can be fun but a little repetitive. Then you see someone on a bike for the first time and think, 'That looks fun!' but perhaps have some apprehension, 'I won't be able to do that; it looks hard.' You are fascinated by this new thing but stick to what you feel comfortable with: your safe, if a little boring, playground.

Then an adult gives you a bike of your own to try. At first, riding it seems impossible; it requires a lot of balance, coordination and skill. You need a supportive adult to help show you how to do it. You need to trust them to keep you safe while you learn. You use stabilisers to build up your confidence and 'get a feel' for what you need to do, then an adult holds your seat while you pedal without stabilisers. Eventually you are pedalling by yourself, alone! You go slow and steady and wobble a bit, but you're doing it! Gradually you build up speed and confidence, until you are cycling without even thinking about it!

You build up your skills over time so you can take on jumps, do tricks and ride over rocky hillsides. You may even enter races to show off your cycling skills or charity bike-rides to push your skills to the next level for a good cause. You can upgrade your bike the better you get. You might enjoy cycling with others now, joining a bike club to share the fun with like-minded people and learning from them.

Finally, you are a competent, and confident, cyclist, taking on new challenges and enjoying your hobby. One day you will teach your kids how to cycle, too.

And in the end, you will achieve *and* have fun!

3. STAYING SAFE WHILE YOU RIDE

Figure 4.5 contrasts the expected life path for perfectionism and optimalism.

How perfectionism thinks life should be   How optimalism knows life will be

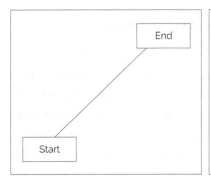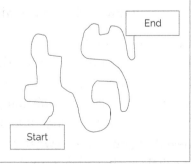

FIGURE 4.5: EXPECTED LIFE PATH FOR PERFECTIONISM AND OPTIMALISM

When you cycle, you wear a helmet in case you fall off, so you don't hurt yourself. You might also wear elbow and knee pads, and gloves or even a body brace, for extra protection. You always carry a water bottle to stay hydrated and quench your thirst. You concentrate hard on the tricky and fast parts of your cycle ride, and relax when coasting along a flat, smooth track. You wear clothes that feel comfortable to cycle in.

When you get even more confident, you might cycle in the dark, using lights to guide your way and keep you safe. You have learned how to do basic safety checks on your bike before you go out; you check the tyres are pumped up and free from punctures, and the brakes work okay. You keep your bike clean after riding so it doesn't get rusty or break, and store it somewhere safe and dry. You get it checked out with a bike mechanic every now and then to make sure it is working properly and get any repairs done. You might even pay money to insure it. Over time, you learn how to service your bike for yourself; you are totally in control and capable. Being a competent cyclist also means being able to judge when it is **not** safe to go out riding, or to stop a bike ride early and re-route. You carry a map in case of such emergencies.

Of course, you can still cycle without all these things, but it is less likely to feel fun as you won't feel safe, so you won't be able to go as fast or try out as many tricks or new routes. It also means that if you do fall off, you are likely to get hurt. And of course cycling in the dark with no lights could be fatal. Cycling after having done all these safety checks means you are taking a calculated risk. Not only will you be a successful cyclist but you will enjoy it too.

Becoming higher in optimalism means knowing what is needed to keep you functioning safely and successfully, and spotting when these things are getting low. Of course, things might still happen that throw you off course or make you wobble; when cycling this might be a sudden rain shower or unexpected pothole; in life this might be a sudden shock or unexpected event. But when you keep looking after your basic needs you are more likely to navigate these successfully, without getting too hurt. And if you do get hurt, it means taking the time to recover properly, and getting back on the bike before you get too scared to try again!

Being high in optimalism also means developing the skill to know when it's not right to begin something new, and when to change direction from something you are already doing; at times in life you need to take a step back from your pursuits and re-evaluate what your priorities are and in which direction you need to head. **Sometimes the most helpful thing to do is to stay still and give yourself time to catch your breath.**

You can plough on through life without looking after your basic needs, but, if you do so, you are at more risk of problems when something does go wrong. Your basic needs include making sure you are well nourished, hydrated, in good physical health through regular exercise and check-ups, have a good sleep regime, somewhere safe to go and a positive social support network around you.

4. Getting messy!

Perfectionism and mess have a love–hate relationship.

Perfectionism is a lot about staying in control, or at least trying to feel as though you are in control. Without the 'mess' of anxiety, there would be no perfectionism. Perfectionism needs anxiety to survive.

When on a roundabout, there's not much chance of getting messy. It is a clean and predictable activity. Riding a roundabout is a good way to avoid getting messy and to stay feeling in control. Unless of course it goes so fast, or you stay on so long that you end up falling off!

When riding a bike, there is a high chance you will get messy. Your legs may get dusty from the dirt tracks, you may get splashed with mud as you cycle through puddles, you may get exhaust fumes in your nostrils from passing traffic, and you may get the occasional leaf or branch in your hair and clothes as you dodge your way through a narrow woodland path! You may even take a tumble and scuff your clothes. And you will almost certainly get hot and sweaty while out on your adventure!

Getting messy is okay. It is 'freeing'. You can clean off again. Clothes can be mended. It is great to have a hot shower or bath after a ride and appreciate how pleasant it feels to get clean and fresh. And there is a real sense of pride in fixing your own bike.

In life, sometimes the thoughts and feelings we have can seem a bit 'messy'. They are hard to make sense of or may embarrass or upset us. At worst, they make us feel ashamed or afraid and we would rather they just went away. Perfectionist behaviours can be a way of trying to keep these thoughts and feelings in order so that the 'messiness' doesn't spill out for others to see.

Thoughts and feelings aren't meant to be pushed away like this! They tend to come back stronger in the future, just like a roundabout getting faster and faster and you feeling unable to slow it down. That, of course, makes it more likely they *will* spill out, but in a way you don't feel in control of. It is helpful to learn to pay more attention to your thoughts and feelings, even if they are uncomfortable or confusing. In fact, *particularly* if they are uncomfortable or confusing. The aim is to eventually do this in a **non-judgemental** way so that they go away on their own without you feeling you are constantly trying to control or escape them.

And once you've noticed them, it is even more important to let them out! The aim is to eventually do this in an **assertive** way so no one gets hurt (including you). When we express our thoughts and feelings we actually end up feeling **calmer and more in control**!

Activities that give you chance to be 'messy' include:

- **Art:** start throwing some paint at a canvas and see what happens! Grab some clay and start to punch and squeeze! There is a list of therapeutic art activities in Appendix C.

- **Creative writing:** let the words flow onto paper without filtering, or write a poem or story to capture your thoughts and feelings.

- **Dance:** move to the sound of your own thoughts! Find music to match for even better effect.

- **Drama:** speak or shout in a different voice or pretend you're someone else – say and do whatever you want!

- **Mindfulness:** do some everyday tasks and notice what thoughts and feelings you have; try to 'stay with' them, however odd or dull they may seem!

- **Music:** grab any instrument you can get hold of and get it to make noise to match how you feel inside! Maybe even add some words.

These activities can help you begin to process some of the more 'messy' thoughts and feelings you might have. Remember, even if you cannot yet make sense of them, it is important to let them out. Another important point to note is that the activities are therapeutic, so there is no 'right' or 'wrong' way to do them! As long as you start to feel calmer and more in control over time, they are working for you.

Becoming high in optimalism feels impossible at first. Perfectionist habits are firmly rooted and can feel comfortable to hang onto, even if being high in optimalism seems more attractive. But with the support of a sensitive adult, you can begin to develop the skills needed to take on life in this more realistic and compassionate way. The skills of optimalism include being able to reframe a mistake as an opportunity to learn and grow, and being able to enjoy the process as much as the outcome.

Action planning

Decide what skill to work on, and plan to address it.

Consider which skill could make your life better, more enjoyable, and bring you more success in areas you value. Now think about how to break down that skill into lots of manageable steps.

For example, if you wanted to express yourself more assertively, a good step towards this might be expressing yourself assertively in a journal, then to a trusted person. It might also be watching someone you consider to be assertive and getting some tips from what they say and do. It could be reading a self-help guide about assertiveness. An unrealistic step would be to be assertive at all times with all people in all situations; this is setting yourself up to fail! Plans need to have carefully thought-through steps towards a goal to make them successful. Finally, consider how and when you are going to get to work on this skill. Ideally, timetable in 'sessions' for this and consider who may be able to help and what, particularly, they can do to support you to develop the skill you want. Remember:

- You need to practise lots to break old habits.

- You will get there with effort and support.

- Once you've got the skills, you'll always have them. Just like riding a bike!

Reflecting on your progress

What went well and what would I do differently next time?

There is limited reflection about one's turn on a roundabout! Perhaps if you fell off you may swear to go slower next time, or to hold on tighter, or to jump off sooner. I wonder if any of those things would bring the same thrill of the ride?

A bike ride offers greater opportunity for reflection: where did you go, which bits were trickier to ride, any obstacles or bumps in the road you have learned about for next time? Which parts brought the most pleasure and therefore you would like to revisit again?

When working on building your skills it is important to reflect on why you are doing it to keep yourself motivated, and to consider what is working well for you that you might like to continue.

Importantly, it is also critical to consider what is not going well so you do not continue to do something that may be causing you more harm than good in the long-run.

Before we launch into the strategies for challenging perfectionism, the next couple of chapters look at systemic considerations. What can we as adults be considering and doing before involving the young person?

Endnotes

1   Tracy and Robins (2004)   2   Yerkes and Dodson (1908)

Chapter 5

Perfectionism within Organisations

'Conform and perform: the move towards a "perfect" world.'

This book would not be complete without a brief reflection on the 'bigger picture'. The child does not develop in a vacuum, but rather as an amalgamation of all the influences around them throughout their childhood and adolescence. This includes their own personality factors, but also their family, their school and neighbourhood communities, the media, government, laws and religion.

There are minimal perfectionism rating scales in use that explicitly mention environmental factors, such as parental expectations and criticism, and teachers expecting perfection.[1] This highlights the dominant 'within-child model' of perfectionism, i.e. the problem is inside the child, therefore the responsibility for change lies with the child. It appears there are *no* measures available to consider the impact on young people of wider environmental factors, such as current media messages, existing laws and trends in public spending. This misses a vital element of the equation.

Lippman (2012) argues that instead of 'problematising perfectionism' and 'pathologising individuals' we should be 'seeking out the societal ills that sparked the problem in the first place'[2] and this reflects a growing movement to focus less on individual responsibility for emotional wellbeing and more on societal responsibility. However, there are mixed messages in society about this idea; these are addressed in brief below.

The quest for perfection and individual responsibility

Over the centuries we as humans have become more efficient in our activities, creating machines to complete work for us meaning we have more time in our day to fill...with more work and responsibilities. Scientists and researchers continue to search for more streamlined, faster, stronger, smaller, quieter versions of machines that will move closer to their vision of 'perfect'.

We have become über-productive. 'Conform and perform' is the powerful message driving high levels of success across many areas of employment. Performance targets are high and performance-related pay is well-established across many workplaces.

In many ways, society is sending the message that it is working towards perfection, aiming for:

- **'The perfect workplace'**, in which employees take minimal breaks, have heightened 'resiliency' to stress, sickness and turnover are reduced, workspaces are optimalised in terms of ergonomics, aesthetics and practicalities, output is maximised, and the organisation fulfils a range of social and charitable duties in terms of its contributions to society and the environment. A range of apparent 'wellbeing' measures may be in place, along with reward systems for 'good work'. Team members get along well in addition to pursuing individual projects that enhance the performance of the company. In health services, waiting times are reduced, 'value for money' is high and 'what could we do better?' pleas are available and acted upon with speed and quality.

- **'The perfect school'**, in which results are consistently high across all areas of learning and behaviour, staff are highly qualified and experienced, school leadership is strong and confident, and no child is left behind. Exclusions are low, the school makes charitable links with the wider community and students go on to a range of Higher Education settings and employers. Parents and governors are satisfied, innovation is celebrated along with 'traditional values' and successful ex-students regularly return to inspire current students. Modern facilities and resources are available and a wide range of opportunities is on offer to all students.

- **'The perfect human'**, in which we are not only finely-tuned workers, but also emotionally stable, able to run a successful home and family life, contribute to charitable organisations and our wider communities, as well as 'bettering ourselves' through ongoing learning and managing to maintain an optimum diet, exercise regime and sleep patterns. We are available to care for elderly relatives and proactively manage our own health so we don't present a similar burden on society when we reach a grand old age.

The flip side of this? The dramatic rise in mental health difficulties over the past few decades.

As the world around us has taken great technological leaps, our 'caveman' brains are struggling to keep up. We are not 'programmed' for such fast-paced, ever-changing lifestyles in which expectations on us are consistently high, in all areas. We are now even expected to have mastered the art of relaxation, becoming expert daily users of mindfulness, meditation and yoga. Although the human brain has evolved impressively over time, we are not the robots required to cope with the demands the world is aiming to place on us, nor will we ever be.

In response to the rise in mental health problems over the past few decades, there has been a spectacular rise in individualised mental health interventions, along with a similar boom in the use of psychotropic medication (e.g. antidepressants).

This is a *reactive* rather than *proactive* response to rising levels of stress, anxiety and depression in our societies. It is also a very *individualised* response, placing the 'blame' for the problem on the individual: *you* are stressed therefore *you* need to have some therapy. *You* feel low therefore *you* need some medication. The *cause* of the problem is within you. Get yourself better, then you can fit back into the regime and be a productive member of society.

Compassion and collective responsibility

There is fortunately another wave of opinion taking shape and strength over the past few years that compassionately considers the wide range of human needs and recognises that the constant pressurised drive to perform is hindering rather than helping progress. This drive towards a 'psychosocial' approach to public mental health aims to prevent problems before they arise through structural changes like social policy and legislation.[3]

This view argues that individual responsibility is *not* the way forward, and in fact may serve to distract us from the bigger problem: cultural and corporate responsibility. So long as we are all focusing on increasing our own resiliency, improving the way we manage stress and ultimately attempting to make our work output better, we are conveniently not looking at the 'bigger picture' and considering the system that is causing the stress in the first place. This is not a new idea; in *A Complete Guide to Therapy* written in 1978, Koval argues that energy should be directed to an overhaul of society rather than placing the focus in the 'individual realm'.[4] Evidently, social change is a challenging feat to accomplish and certainly takes time.

Relating to perfectionism, an example of social change is the slow but positive move away from the 'perfect person' used in advertising and marketing campaigns. Many companies are now choosing models of varying size, age, gender, ethnicity, sexuality, ability and other qualities rather than one stereotypical person to represent their product or service. This is a step in the right direction in terms of the messages received by our young people about who they are expected to be in order to fit in, succeed and be happy in our society.

- Can you think of other examples of the media, or laws, changing to reflect the diversity of society rather than providing us with an 'ideal' or unrealistic presentation?

- What changes have you noticed that recognise our wellbeing needs as well as society's need for progress?

There are fortunately many, however there is still much to be done.

One problem with individual intervention is that it will never be available to everyone who needs it,[5] and also that it focuses on being reactive rather than proactive in solving problems, leading to high levels of stress amongst psychotherapists[6] and 'relapses' for those accessing treatment. The 'cause' of many people's mental health difficulties, or at least a major trigger, is outside themselves, in their work and personal lives. Relating to children, Paul Gilbert (2002) suggested that instead of campaigning to 'defeat depression' by raising children's resiliency, we should instead campaign to 'defeat abuse' by preventing the childhood sexual abuse that triggers depression in some children.[7] In the same way, instead of entirely focusing on reducing perfectionism in young people, we need to consider the influences within society that are inspiring the perfectionist attitudes in the first place.

We are in an interesting point in history in which we have the most incredible technology available to us and resources for improving this even further, and our greatest ever awareness of emotional wellbeing and how best to enhance this. The two do not always get along. How society resolves this conflict will be pivotal in ensuring success *and* happiness for the population. An 'optimalist' approach is likely to be key in achieving this balance.

Ways forward

Change is hard, yet we frequently expect it of young people. This book supports the need for early systemic intervention to help *prevent* a range of later problems. The first place we can start to make an impact on the mixed messages in our society is to consider our own beliefs, attitudes and behaviours which are likely to be influencing our young people.

Questions we as adults need to be asking ourselves:

- Are student's expectations of themselves reasonable?

- Are ours? Young people learn how to 'be' from observing us.

- What about the expectations on us, as parents, as educators: how are these influencing our thoughts, feelings and behaviours?

- Is it possible in our environment to be 'good enough' or is this not acceptable? What messages is this giving us and our young people? What does it mean to be a 'good-enough' parent or teacher?

- What is the cost – personal, financial, etc – of making mistakes in our society? What is the message being conveyed about avoidance of mistakes and instead aiming for a 'perfect' performance?

- How is our emotional wellbeing supported as parents and school staff? If we do not feel emotionally contained, validated and secure, how can we expect our young people to do so?

- Is it okay in our society to be different, to voice controversial opinions, to behave in ways congruent with our values even if they are not the social norm? Or is conformity the only real way to behave?

These attitudes and beliefs will shape the things we say and do. Frequently as adults we unwittingly say things intended to motivate and encourage our young people, but which may in fact be reinforcing unhelpful perfectionist beliefs.

See Table 5.1 for examples of these everyday comments and what could be said instead to promote a healthier, more 'optimalist' attitude in our young people.

Table 5.1: Things to say that reinforce perfectionism or encourage optimalism

Perfectionism-reinforcing	Message received by/thoughts of child	Optimalism-encouraging	Message received by/thoughts of child
'Always try your best.'	What, always? That's exhausting. How can I keep this up?	'Put in lots of effort when it's really needed.'	Sometimes I need to try as best as I can, but other times it's okay to just do 'good enough'.
'Work as hard as you can and you'll achieve it.'	If I work hard enough I will be successful. I must work hard.	'Work smart and you'll achieve it.'	If I think carefully about what I need to do, get help and do enough practice I can succeed.
'You didn't win because it was fixed/they cheated.'	If I don't win everyone else is to blame.	'You didn't win because they did better than you on the day.'	Sometimes I win, sometimes I don't and that's okay.
'Don't be over-sensitive/ridiculous/silly.'	My feelings are unimportant, silly and a nuisance. I need to keep them hidden away.	'It's okay to feel worried, frustrated or disappointed about that. It shows you care and will motivate you to do things differently next time.'	My feelings are valid and an important message to learn from.
'You made me drop that, don't get in my way'; 'Haha, she muddled her words, she looks so silly now'; 'Oh no, you got two wrong, what a shame!'	Mistakes are bad. My mistakes will be noticed and laughed at. It is not okay to make mistakes. I need to be perfect.	'Oops, I made a mistake! Never mind, I will do it differently next time'; 'Oh wow look, she really improved'; 'You got most of them right; you must've concentrated really well this time, great job.'	I can improve over time and learn from my mistakes. Mistakes are okay and help me make progress.

cont.

Perfectionism-reinforcing	Message received by/thoughts of child	Optimalism-encouraging	Message received by/thoughts of child
'You're really clever/smart/funny, etc.; I'm no good at that.'	That is who I am as a person. I need to keep showing that. You either are those things, or you are not.	'You looked really carefully at that/learned from your mistake/made a funny connection that made us laugh. I struggle with that but I could learn from you, practise and get better.'	The things I do help me in my life. I can repeat them if I want, and even improve them. I can help others to learn. We can all improve.
'Don't do that; it'll take too much time and effort. You've never done it before so you'll struggle. Stick with what you're good at.'	New things are to be avoided. Effort is a bad thing. If something feels hard, stay away.	'That sounds like a new challenge; it may take a bit of time and energy to figure out what to do, but it might be worth it!'	It's okay to try new things and to put in effort. It is okay to find things hard; this means my brain is growing.

In Appendix D there is an article from Oxford High School for Girls which reflects on a whole-school approach to tackling perfectionism, recognising some of the systemic influences on young people. The Deputy Headteacher who initiated this project, based on her background in developmental psychology, psychiatry research and education, had noticed increasingly worrying signs of perfectionism in the students and wanted to do something proactive to tackle this. Examples of activities the school carried out include a whole-school assembly, cognitive-behavioural coaching, trying a new skill (a Capella singing) and having visits from people working in Higher Education. The school observed hopeful results from this project and strongly encourage other schools to try similar initiatives. The Deputy Headteacher's wider reflections on the project, gathered through an interview and written correspondence, are also available in Appendix D.

Process- or target-driven?

When speaking with our young people we want to reinforce the optimalist messages:

- It is okay to feel a range of emotions.

- It is okay to find things hard and put in effort.

- It is okay to make mistakes.

- It is okay to try new things.

All these messages help a student become more *process*- and less *target*-driven. This offers great benefits in terms of their learning and wellbeing.

This may sound reasonably straightforward; however, consider ways in which the 'end point' is reinforced in our schools and society:

- examination results and performance-related pay for teachers

- celebration assemblies and prize-giving for achievement

- Olympic medals for 'the best' in sport

- cash bonuses for 'the best' in business

- awards for 'the best' in film, music and television.

Consider also the ways in which mistakes and failings are highlighted in society and schools:

- the news items reported on television and in newspapers

- 'bloopers' and outtakes television shows

- social media memes and celebrity stories in magazines.

Can you think of ways in which the process and journey are celebrated? Or ways in which society validates making and learning from mistakes as a valuable part of progress?

How does your family/school celebrate effort, enjoying the moment and learning from mistakes?

We must be careful we are not only rewarding the 'end point' with our young people. Often this is unintentional and learned from the messages around us in society. If we stop and think about what we are doing, we can be more mindful about the messages we are conveying to our young people.

Consider the following statements:

- A satisfactory teacher will ensure students achieve success at school.

- A good teacher will ensure students achieve success in school and the likelihood of success later on.

- An excellent teacher will help students develop the skills to ensure both their own success **and** happiness in **and beyond** school.

To what extent do you agree with these statements?

We all have our own views about the purpose and function of school. What are yours? What are the young person's?

The following chapter addresses strategies at both an individual *and* systemic level, albeit on the level of school staff and families. The bigger mission of changing things at increasingly higher levels is a work in progress! We can begin with our own lives and the attitudes and behaviours within our workplace and homes. I hope you find some benefit in the pages ahead, and also feel inspired and empowered to make changes where possible to help create a more 'optimalist' world.

Endnotes

1 Frost Multidimensional Perfectionism Scale (FMPS) (Frost *et al.* 1990) and Child-Adolescent Perfectionism Scale (CAPS) (Flett *et al.* 2016)

2 Lippman (2012, p.3)

3 Harper (2016)

4 Koval (1978, p.14)

5 Harper (2016)

6 British Psychological Society (2016)

7 Gilbert (2002)

Chapter 6

Moving from Perfectionism towards Optimalism

'From survive, to thrive: the real possibility
of success and happiness.'

Now we have learned about what perfectionism is (and is not), considered how we might identify if a young person is high in perfectionism and why we should be concerned, discussed the need to move towards a more 'optimalist' way of living and reflected on wider societal and cultural pressures and expectations, we can now explore what to target for change and how to put in place strategies to encourage this.

This chapter is based upon the existing international research on perfectionism, combined with my own knowledge and experience from my training, research and career to date.

What the research says

It is notable that in their 2014 review of the childhood perfectionism literature, Morris and Lomax identified 84 eligible studies regarding psychopathology (i.e. the 'problem' of perfectionism), but only seven regarding treatment. This highlights the current state of perfectionism research and the need for a greater, solution-focused approach to address the identified problem. Encouragingly, Lloyd and colleagues' systematic review and meta-analysis of the adult treatment literature in 2015 positively concluded that psychological interventions *can* reduce perfectionism and associated difficulties. Summarised below is the minimal research into interventions for overcoming childhood perfectionism.

Psychoeducation

This is a therapeutic approach that raises awareness and understanding of the issue and teaches self-help skills for overcoming problematic thinking and behaving. It may be a helpful approach in schools to enable students to share their experiences and concerns without fear of judgement. 'Bibliotherapy' (the use of story/text to aid healing) and the use of cartoons have been found to engage younger students and increase their comprehension of perfectionism.[1] Web-based psychoeducational interventions appear promising for older students.[2] However, psychoeducation has been found to be ineffective when used as a standalone intervention in adult populations,[3] highlighting the need for early intervention and a more integrative approach.

Cognitive-Behavioural Therapy (CBT)

This is a therapeutic approach that helps individuals recognise irrational thinking about personal standards and mistake-making, encouraging more realistic expectations of themselves and finding alternative ways to approach situations. When perfectionism is the specific target of the therapy, rather than part of a general programme, CBT can successfully reduce perfectionism in older students and adults.[4] Face-to-face or guided self-help are thought to be more effective than pure online self-help[5] for older students, and the use of groupwork may also be beneficial.[6] It is unknown whether such approaches would work with younger students, although there is increasing evidence to suggest that CBT approaches in general may be beneficial for school students.[7]

Other therapeutic approaches

There is support for the use of narrative and play therapy techniques for addressing perfectionism, using a high level of liaison between parents and teachers.[8] The following psychotherapeutic approaches have also shown some value with students high in perfectionism; Acceptance and Commitment Therapy,[9] Quality of Life Therapy,[10] Coherence Therapy,[11] Cognitive Remediation Therapy[12] and a cognitive pastoral approach employing narcissistic personality disorder strategies.[13] The 'third wave' of psychotherapies (e.g. Mindfulness Based Cognitive Therapy, Multimodal Therapy, Metacognitive Therapy, Schema Therapy, Dialectical Behaviour Therapy), if targeted specifically at perfectionist thoughts, feelings and behaviours, may be an area for further exploration for addressing perfectionism in young people, as these approaches are increasingly recognised to be effective in addressing depression, anxiety and stress in young people, all of which have links with perfectionism.

Curriculum approaches

Lead perfectionism researchers Flett and Hewitt (2008, 2014) argue for a universal, school-based, proactive intervention to build competencies such as enhancing resilience, coping and self-regulation and reducing levels of perfectionism by addressing students' sense of responsibility and self-criticism. Nugent (2000) offers practical ideas for improving coping skills at a universal level, including bibliotherapy, art activities and group therapeutic discussion. Guerra and Bradshaw (2008) highlighted 'core competencies' they felt were beneficial for promoting the wellbeing of young people high in perfectionism. These are:

- a positive sense of self

- self-control

- decision-making skills

- a moral system of belief

- prosocial connectedness.

As already mentioned in Chapter 5, the Oxford High School for Girls ran a whole-school CBT-based campaign they entitled 'Goodbye Little Miss Perfect' using work by Shafran, Egan and Wade (2010) to proactively address school-based pressures and promote self-compassion as a substitute for self-criticism. Although not formally evaluated, this offers a starting point for school-based approaches. An account of this campaign written by the Deputy Headteacher at the time, with her reflections on the approach, can be found in Appendix D.

An eclectic mix

Perfectionism is not as 'black-or-white' as it may first appear, so perhaps it is fitting that the ideal interventions are also not so clear-cut. Students high in perfectionism are all individuals, and the school setting and home environments they belong to are also unique. Interventions to support such students may require a more holistic approach than simply addressing either individual 'treatment' or whole-school cultural change. Mofield and Chakraborti-Ghosh (2010) feel that perfectionism is a sign that the student is experiencing difficulty coping, so coping skills should be universally improved for *all* students then a targeted affective curriculum can be provided for those students particularly high in perfectionism, with a strong focus on classroom culture and parent involvement. This supports Rimm's (2007) long-term American study which argued for both a systemic and individual approach.

What follows in the next two chapters are my 'ABC' strategies based on a thorough examination of the existing literature on perfectionism, including the existing interventions for both children and adults, and reflections on a range of therapeutic approaches with which I am familiar from my professional training and experience. The strategies are primarily based around the principles of Acceptance and Commitment Therapy, Cognitive Behavioural Therapy, and Dialectical Behaviour Therapy, integrating elements of these approaches to aim to suit a range of young people. Their application to perfectionism is summarised below.

ACCEPTANCE AND COMMITMENT THERAPY (ACT)

This approach uses mindfulness and metaphor to develop acceptance of difficulties and behaviour-change strategies based upon individual areas of value. It is a compassionate approach that aims to be present with what life brings (rather than trying to eliminate difficult feelings) and move closer to more valued behaviours. It is a good match for perfectionism as it aims to develop a young person's awareness and acceptance of their own strengths and needs, and help them to develop clarity about their identity and goals. A particular benefit of ACT for perfectionism is its power to increase flexibility and tolerance of distress.

COGNITIVE-BEHAVIOURAL THERAPY (CBT)

This approach increases awareness of how thoughts, beliefs and attitudes affect feelings and behaviour. It teaches coping skills for managing different problems such as anxiety, stress and low mood. It is a good match for perfectionism as it specifically targets the 'cognitive errors' typically present for students high in perfectionism. It also aims to help the young person identify feelings and respond to these in more helpful ways. A particular benefit of CBT for perfectionism is its power to break the cycle created by perfectionist thoughts.

DIALECTICAL BEHAVIOUR THERAPY (DBT)

This approach is an adapted form of CBT that helps people who experience emotions very intensely and who are likely to engage in 'addictive' behaviours in an attempt to manage these, such as self-harm and substance abuse. It is a good match for perfectionism as it recognises the difficulties in changing and the use of behaviours as a way of coping, as well as being aimed at people who see the world in 'black-or-white' terms. It aims to help the young person learn to recognise and tolerate a range of distressing feelings, as well as teaching healthy ways to get their needs met. A particular benefit of DBT for perfectionism is its balance between acceptance and change.

The principles of intervention

Intervention works best when it follows an ASSESS–PLAN–DO–REVIEW cycle. This can be found in Appendix E. We have already considered how to 'assess' if a young person needs support in Chapter 1 through identifying the types of thoughts, feelings and behaviours that may be a cause for concern and considering what the underlying unmet need may be. We will now address the remaining parts of this intervention structure.

Planning for change – 'PLAN'

Let us first consider the ideal target for intervention. Figure 6.1 highlights three different areas on which you could focus, with the corresponding likelihood of lasting change.

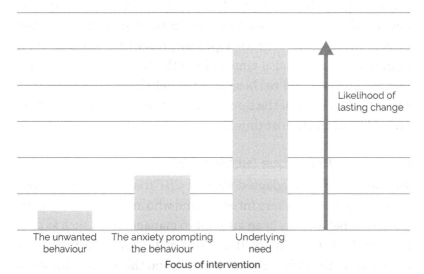

FIGURE 6.1: TARGETS FOR INTERVENTION FOR LASTING CHANGE

Interventions focusing on general stress management, body image or coping with anxiety **do not** have a beneficial or lasting effect on perfectionism. What is required is a specific focus on perfectionism as a *coping skill to manage the anxiety of an unmet need*, and therefore a combination of:

- developing a healthy range of alternative coping skills to manage anxiety

- targeting the underlying need.

How can I help my young person be more optimalist and less perfectionist?

Our aim is to develop the coping skills of the young person to help reduce the anxiety underlying perfectionism.

Start by asking yourself the following questions:

1. What are the specific skills you/the young person would like the young person to learn? E.g.:

    - problem-solving

    - making decisions

    - self-esteem

    - assertive communication

    - making and following through plans

    - recognising emotions

    - managing and expressing emotions

    - recovering from emotional highs and lows

    - developing and maintaining positive, healthy relationships

    - optimism

    - adaptability

- tolerance of imperfection

- managing a range of sensory input.

2. Where are they now with these skills? (e.g. rate on a scale 0–10 for each skill, and describe in words)

3. What are the steps between 1 and 2, i.e. where they are now and where you would like them to be? Break down this journey into as many small steps as possible so it feels more achievable.

4. What activities can you think of that could help the student achieve each step? Be creative! Home and school can work together on this for maximum impact.

What are the goals of intervention?

As previously highlighted, young people high in perfectionism are likely to lack helpful coping strategies, and instead use perfectionist behaviours as a way to feel in control. Even if this seems to be working for them, research suggests they may become 'unstuck' later in life when these strategies cannot compete with the responsibilities and demands of adulthood and the 'real world'.

There are therefore two main goals of intervention:

1. the young person develops awareness of their own perfectionist thoughts and behaviours and the problems associated with perfectionism

2. the young person develops more adaptive ways of thinking and behaving, considering cognitive, behavioural, emotional and interpersonal aspects of perfectionism.

In order to achieve these goals, young people must experience the following environment and adult approach:

1. **safe**, **relaxed** and **supportive** so young person feels able to take risks and make mistakes

2. **process** and **effort** are valued as much as (or more than) achievement and outcome

3. young people know what a 'healthy high achiever' looks like through your explicit **role-modelling**.

We can only take risks if we feel able to **cope**, both with the process (i.e. tolerating **not** always having control over things) and with the potential outcome (i.e. tolerating **not** always having things a certain or expected way). Developing our coping skills relies, in part, on recognising our own **needs**.

General targets for young people high in perfectionism are therefore likely to be:

1. recognising and managing emotions in a healthy way

2. strengthening the self: promoting self-acceptance and self-compassion to counter self-criticism

3. prosocial connectedness

4. seeing failures as pathways to success: attributional reframing and fostering a growth mindset to enable better decision-making and problem-solving skills

5. lowering standards and the importance of being perfect.[14]

You may, of course, want to set more specific goals to meet individual needs (e.g. recognising and managing anger, building up a relationship with a key member of staff, learning through mistakes in maths lessons, etc.).

What to do if you are concerned about a young person – 'DO'

See Appendix F for a flowchart of different options for different situations, which are explained in more detail below.

Young person acknowledges problem

If the young person recognises and accepts there is a problem, they may be amenable to individual or groupwork in school, or perhaps may benefit from the expertise of outside professionals. This will be down to the professional judgement of staff as to whether the needs can be met at school level. Discussions should include the young person, who may have a clear preference for the type of support they would like. These preferences should be accommodated as far as is reasonable. Chapters 7 and 8 provide some ideas for strategies for adults and the young person to use.

Young person does not acknowledge problem

If the young person seems unaware or resistant to the idea of their thoughts, feelings or behaviours being problematic, it may be best to operate a systemic, universal approach, unless you have serious concerns about their mental health or learning in which case it would be wise to request the involvement of external professionals, such as an educational/school psychologist. The young person's behaviour and progress should be monitored and liaison with parents take place where appropriate to ensure a collaborative approach. You can begin to raise the young person's self-awareness through gentle and cautious reflections which enable them to increase their motivation to change at a pace that feels comfortable for them. Chapter 7 provides some ideas for strategies adults can use that do not require the young person to acknowledge the problem.

School-based support

Depending on the young person and practicalities within school, support may take the form of 1:1 sessions, group sessions, or holding meetings with the family and young person to discuss matters openly. Again, Chapters 7 and 8 provide strategies that can be discussed in these forums.

External support

Advice may be sought from local child and adolescent mental health services or the school/educational psychologist if they have capacity to offer support with this. They may want to work with the young person, their family and/or yourselves. The greater the impact on the young person's functioning, the more this option should be pursued. External professionals may also need to be contacted if an underlying need is identified that requires support in addition to what can be provided in school, e.g. Occupational Therapist, Speech and Language Therapist, Autism/ Communication Advisory Teacher, etc.

Systemic support

A whole-school approach can be adopted to challenge perfectionist ways of thinking and behaving amongst the whole school community. Please see Appendix D for the example from the Oxford High School for Girls. Chapter 7 also discusses some whole-school strategies.

In all situations

Try to keep the young person at the centre of discussions and remember they are coping as best they can with the skills, knowledge and understanding they currently have. It is wise to keep accurate records of any concerns, conversations and actions carried out with young people and families. These may be useful for future reference or in discussion with external professionals. Remember to respect confidentiality and follow your safeguarding policy. For your own emotional wellbeing it may be valuable to ensure you have time to 'debrief' your experiences formally or informally with colleagues or an external professional. Parents/ carers requiring additional support may benefit from discussions with their family doctor, local social care teams or through their own counselling.

The principles of support

It is important to remember that behaviour does not change overnight, particularly well-ingrained behaviours like perfectionism, where there are likely to be perceived benefits (e.g. sense of control, achievement). In this sense, we have to remember that perfectionism is comparable to an addiction! It will take time, practice, and adult understanding and support, recognising that the student is on a journey through the stages of change[15] which is likely to require patience and understanding.

It is important to consider **balance** when working with students high in perfectionism. This is because there are a number of *dialectics* (equal and seemingly opposing ideas) involved which require sophisticated thinking to understand and model for young people. We are working to help the young person resolve the conflict between these opposing ideas and to feel more comfortable in the 'middle ground', or what is known in Dialectical Behaviour Therapy as 'Wise Mind'. We want life to feel less 'all-or-nothing', 'black-or-white' and for them to find, and become more comfortable with, the space in between the extremes. These conflicting messages are shown in Figure 6.2.

FIGURE 6.2: BALANCING 'DIALECTICS'

Another important point to note is that not all adults will feel comfortable in offering emotional support to young people. This is okay! Pastoral skills can be learned just as things like behaviour management and ICT skills can. There are books, websites, training courses and other forms of support out there if you need to improve your skills in emotional literacy and support. There is no shame in this; they do not come naturally to everyone. Just as with other areas of learning, some of us need more teaching and practice than others.

Balance, flexibility and compassion are key components of challenging perfectionism; as adults we must remember to apply these things to ourselves as well.

Reflecting on the support – 'REVIEW'

The final part of the intervention cycle is to 'review' how things are going. This can be as informal as your own reflections on what is happening for the young person and what seems to be helpful (or unhelpful), to a more formal meeting involving all key adults and perhaps the young person themselves, in which someone takes notes and everyone receives a copy.

The key considerations for this part of the process are the following:

- What is the current situation and how does it compare to where we were at the beginning? Have there been any improvements? Has anything got worse?

- Are we clear about what the young person's needs are? (Your view might have changed having started the process.)

- What seems to be helping or going well? Why might this be?

- Has anything been unhelpful or made things worse? Why might this be?

- What are we going to do next? What will we continue, what will we stop? Do we need to involve anyone else? What skills do we want to work on?

It is helpful to set a further date to review what is happening, otherwise interventions can 'fizzle out'. Knowing you are going to look closely at what has been happening on a certain date helps to focus people's attention on the intervention and ensure they are doing what they can to make it work.

An important point to note is that the deeper impact of this work may not become apparent until much later, maybe once the young person has left school. Of course, this is harder to then 'measure'. The Deputy Headteacher of Oxford High School for Girls reflected on this point following the whole-school project:

> the impact of any intervention at school may not be evident within the school years (I tried to measure impact of our 'intervention', and collected some data, but long-term impact will, I suspect, be far more important, yet difficult to ascertain!). When I've had conversations with parents about this, I've found that they identified with the suggestion that we would need to ask students in ten or 20 years' time if they felt our work around perfectionism had had an impact.

Applying an 'optimalist' attitude to this cycle, remember:

- No one is expecting a 'perfect' result; change takes time and does not always happen 'in a straight line'. Progress can halt, people can 'regress'. We are looking for a general trend in a positive direction over time.

- The intervention can be reviewed again and again and again, and as many changes made as necessary to find what works for the young person. Sometimes it can be just as helpful to find the things that *don't* work.

- It is okay for the process to feel frustrating, anxiety provoking or even hopeless at times. These are valid feelings, and they will pass. Keep reminding yourself of the targets and celebrate any progress along the way (including 'keeping going' instead of 'giving up').

- Look after your own wellbeing throughout.

The next two chapters describe each of the 'ABC' strategies in more detail, for adults to use with young people (Chapter 7), then for the young people to use themselves, if ready to do so (Chapter 8).

Endnotes

1   e.g. Zousel, Rule and Logan (2013)

2   e.g. Arpin-Cribbie *et al.* (2008)

3   e.g. Steele *et al.* (2013)

4   e.g. Coughlin and Kalodner (2006); Pleva and Wade (2007)

5   Egan *et al.* (2014)

6   e.g. Kearns, Forbes and Gardiner (2007); Kutlesa and Arthur (2008)

7   e.g. Greig and Mackay (2013); Squires (2001)

8   Ashby, Kottman and Martin (2004); Daigneault (1999)

9   Szymanski (2011)

10 Padash, Moradi and Saadat (2014)

11 Rice, Neimeyer and Taylor (2011)

12 Whitney, Easter and Tchanturia (2008)

13 Pembroke (2012)

14 Adapted from Flett and Hewitt (2014) 'A proposed framework for preventing perfectionism' and Guerra and Bradshaw (2008) 'Core competencies for positive youth development and risk prevention'.

15 Prochaska and DiClemente (1983)

Chapter 7

Strategies for Adults Working with Young People

'Great progress can be made by taking one small step at a time.'

Ready...

As perfectionism appears to develop within the context of relationships and involves cognitive and emotional processes, it makes sense that interventions for perfectionism reflect this. Based on psychological theories, a range of therapeutic approaches, research and practice, here is an 'ABC' framework of strategies designed to help adults to support young people high in perfectionism to move towards something healthier: optimalism. They have been written as 'ABCs' to help reduce a complicated topic to something that hopefully feels more straightforward and accessible. There is also a 'quick guide' summary of strategies following the 'ABCs' which combines the support discussed in this book into broad themes for quick reference, followed by a 'whole-school approach' with suggested activities. The chapter concludes with a reminder of the importance of regularly reviewing your support for the young person.

Set...

Perfectionism is not simple; it arises and is maintained in a complex way, therefore we must be mindful that challenging perfectionism is also complex. It will take time, patience, perseverance and effort. Employing your knowledge and understanding gained through what you have read so far, and the 'ABC' strategies, will help make challenging perfectionism feel more achievable.

I thoroughly recommend approaching these strategies with optimalism:

- ✓ You do not have to remember or try all these things.

- ✓ Even if you just try out one or two, that will be a positive move in the right direction.

- ✓ It is better to try, even if you feel unsuccessful, than not to try at all. Making mistakes is an important part of learning and even though they may feel unpleasant, you can take something from the experience to make things even better next time. The young person needs you to at least try.

- ✓ Start small and work up.

- ✓ Ask for help in a way in which you feel comfortable to do so.

- ✓ Remember change is possible with time, practice and opportunity.

Please note that the more of the strategies that are in place, the more likely a young person is to move towards an optimalist mindset and away from destructive perfectionist tendencies. However even trying out one or two could have a positive impact!

Go!

The ABCs are shown in Table 7.1 and explained in more detail over the following pages.

Table 7.1: The 'ABCs' of challenging perfectionism

A	B	C
Acceptance	Balance	Communication
Attention	Boundaries	Challenge
Advice	Behaviour	Coping
Attitude	Beliefs	Compassion
Assertiveness	Bibliotherapy	Choice

A-strategies

Acceptance

'You are enough.'

✓ Ask yourself: do you value, welcome and accept the *whole* person and not just one or two aspects of them? How do you show this? What are the parts you comment on most? These are likely to take on the most significance for your young person. Start to actively notice and respond to different qualities of the young person.

✓ Model having both strengths and needs: parts of yourself you like and parts you wish you could change. This is being human and is a powerful message to model for your young person. We **all** have strengths **and** needs. Show the ability to embrace our 'flaws' and 'limitations' as a way of fully accepting ourselves for who we are.

✓ Place more emphasis on acceptance of how things are than on change. You accept the young person exactly as they are. Paradoxically, this tends to spark motivation and energy to achieve, progress and change! When the focus is all about change and not about accepting who the young person currently is, this leads to a state of anxiety which actually prevents real and positive change. A feeling of **genuine** acceptance provides a sense of calm from which the young person can grow.

✓ What is important to the young person? What do they value?

Do you give this/these things enough attention, encouragement, praise? Find ways to acknowledge the things that are important to them, even if they are not important to you. For example, the football team they support, their interest in bird watching/ Tudor novels/collecting a particular brand of toy, their choice of clothes... This is part of accepting the young person for who they are, not what they do. It will help them develop a more stable and positive identity.

✓ Does the young person have a helpful role model in their life, someone like them with whom they can identify? If they are surrounded by people they are expected to be like, but with whom they struggle to identify, this will be anxiety provoking. Can you find a member of the community, family friend, book or film character you can introduce to help the young person develop greater self-acceptance? The message you want to convey is, 'It is okay to be you!'

Attention

'You are important.'

✓ Do you give the young person positive attention for a range of different areas of their development, their character, their actions? Spend a week noticing what you comment on and 'reward' with your attention (good or bad). Is this the area you want the young person to develop, at the expense of others? Try to start giving attention to other areas of their life too.

✓ Some 'quality time' together can go a long way in conveying this message, and is more valuable than your gifts, money or promises to a young person. Make time regularly to **genuinely** listen to what the young person has to say, give opportunity for them to share any concerns and just find ways to enjoy each other's company; for example, by engaging in a pleasurable activity together. I would thoroughly advise switching off your mobile phone for the duration; young people are very good at noticing when your attention is elsewhere.

✓ Look online to find Dr Daniel Siegel's 'Healthy Mind Platter'.[1] Use this image to try to give more balanced attention to all aspects of the young person (their sleep, physical activity, connecting with others and the natural world, time to reflect, play, focus and downtime). Work towards modelling this yourself, as the young person will learn a lot from observing your lifestyle.

Advice

'You can seek help when you need it.'

✓ Do you help the young person with important life skills such as managing their feelings, handling complex social situations and developing self-organisation? If you can't help with these things, find someone who can or look into resources to support the young person with these things. We all need guidance, sometimes, to develop key skills.

✓ Model seeking advice and guidance when needed so the young person has a model for how to do this, and the message that 'it is okay to seek support'. Show the young person how to do this for more simple, everyday tasks as well as waiting for 'an emergency' or crisis to seek help.

Attitude

'You have a growth mindset.'

✓ Young people learn from watching and listening to you. Consider and reflect upon your own mindset, modelled through your words and actions (F = fixed mindset; G = growth mindset):

• Do you see learning as a struggle (F) or an adventure (G)?

• Do you see new experiences as overwhelming and to be avoided (F), or as challenges to be embraced (G)?

• Do you see mistakes as pathways to development and growth (G), or as signs you are not good enough, a failure and should give up (F)?

- Do you see emotions as a sign you are human and an important way to understand your experiences (G), or an annoyance or sign of weakness that must be hidden or extinguished (F)?

✓ Challenge yourself to reframe your automatic thoughts if they are suggesting a more 'fixed' mindset; for example, 'I'll never be able to do that' becomes 'I can improve with practice'; 'I need to look flawless' becomes 'Good enough is good enough' and 'It's too hard; it's not worth doing' becomes 'Challenges and effort help me grow.' We want to model a strong growth mindset to our young people to help them develop more optimalist ways of being. The attitude we are modelling is 'we can change, we can grow, we can learn' and that 'mistakes and emotions are a valuable and necessary part of being human'.

✓ Remind the young person frequently that no one is perfect and it is okay not to be. The more the young person hears this, in a relaxed, positive and confident tone from the adults around them, the more likely they will be to internalise the message. Reinforce the message that effort is more important than perfection. Ensure you model this also, as the young person is constantly learning from watching as well as listening to you.

✓ Make sure you are not accidentally reinforcing perfectionism by showering them in praise for any achievements. We want to reinforce the effort put in and risks taken in their learning, rather than the final product. An example is going out for a celebratory meal once a project is completed and handed in, or at the end of a day of tests, rather than waiting until you hear the results. Another example is simply telling them how proud you are of them for trying something new even though they felt nervous.

Assertiveness

'You can get your needs met without upsetting anyone.'

✓ Does the young person know how to express their thoughts and feelings and get their needs met assertively? This is a skill that many people spend a lifetime developing! Do you model assertiveness? Does the young person spend time with assertive people? We want to avoid them being passive, aggressive, or passive-aggressive, which are all ways of communicating that either cause some harm to the young person and/or the people around them. Assertiveness is a happy medium and is a communication skill that can be developed. It involves expressing yourself without getting upset or upsetting others. Model this for the young person and help them develop the skill for themselves.

✓ Consider book, TV or film characters that stand up for themselves without becoming upset or upsetting others. Consider characters also who communicate aggressively, or who remain passive and do not get their needs met. Share these with the young person and encourage them to reflect on what works well and what does not.

B-strategies

Balance

**'You spend your time and effort on
different areas of your life.'**

✓ Does the young person have a healthy mixture of work, leisure, relaxation, social time and exercise? Do you? Young people learn how to structure their time and efforts by observing the adults around them. See Dr Daniel Siegel's 'Healthy Mind Platter' and start to work towards obtaining a balance in your daily routines. If any areas are lacking, introduce these slowly and work together on making them enjoyable. If a young person is 'overdoing it' in many areas, consider ways in which these can be 'stripped back' to their most important elements.

✓ Does the young person understand what is meant by balance? What do they understand when they hear phrases like 'do your best' or 'try your hardest'? For someone high in optimalism, this means 'working conscientiously for a reasonable amount of time'. For someone high in perfectionism it may mean 'working on it until it's perfect'. Teach them what 'good enough' actually means and looks like in reality, and reinforce the message that they do not have to do things perfectly in order to succeed. Help them to find a balance over time between their idea of 'success' and 'failure'.

Boundaries

'You set yourself reasonable limits.'

✓ Can the young person set themselves appropriate boundaries? Do they see you setting appropriate boundaries on your time, efforts, behaviours, etc? Try to set limits on tasks so they do not drag on, impinging on time that could be used for other important things. Setting a timer can be helpful, or having a timetable to follow to make sure you keep an overview of what needs to be done. 'That's enough' is a helpful mantra to repeat as needed. It may be useful to have a tray or box where they can safely put anything unfinished to return to later, rather than always needing to get to the end of a task. 'To-do' lists can be helpful, if not 'overdone'; model how to make these work for you. You are the master, not the slave, of a 'to-do' list.

✓ Try to help the young person distinguish between what is **necessary**, and what is extra or optional. Help them develop a 'good enough' mindset by supporting them to focus on the **purpose** of a task. For example, it is often the content of a piece of work that will receive the majority of the marks, not its presentation. The 'success criteria' are helpful things to consider before starting a task, i.e. what specifically is needed to achieve the task. The young person could make a note of these and be encouraged to refer to them regularly.

Behaviour

'You do things to challenge yourself.'

✓ Does the young person try out different ways of behaving to try to get different outcomes? It can be easy to become stuck with familiar ways of behaving. Notice the behaviours you think may be unhelpful in the long term and consider what behaviours you would like the young person to do **instead** of these.

✓ The way we behave can affect the way we think, just as the way we think can affect the way we behave. Support the young person to do things differently and reflect upon what they might now think about the same situation. The more they behave differently, the more their thoughts are likely to change. This will set up a helpful cycle of thinking and behaving to replace their less helpful cycle.

✓ Do you celebrate the moments when the young person steps out of their comfort zone? It can be useful to create a visual record of the young person's progress, such as photographs on a mobile phone or cuttings from a magazine or newspaper stuck into a journal to represent what the young person has accomplished in terms of changing their behaviour. Take time with the young person to reflect on their progress and to help them see that learning is a process rather than a single event.

✓ Are there any of your behaviours you would like to change or that the young person has commented upon? Take the opportunity to try out new ways of behaving that model to the young person that change is possible and survivable.

Beliefs

'You believe in yourself.'

✓ Do you think the young person thinks about themselves, other people and the world in helpful or unhelpful ways? Beliefs can be evident through things the young person says or the things they do. Try to work out what the young person might believe about themselves, other people and life in general from observing them in different situations. If any are less helpful, consider what you would prefer them to be replaced with.

✓ Try to reinforce helpful beliefs, such as 'I am able to solve problems'; 'Other people are helpful when I am stuck' and 'Life is generally fair if I am kind and put in effort.'

✓ Try to challenge the unhelpful beliefs, e.g. 'I should be able to get this first time'; 'Other people are waiting to see me fail and laugh at me', and 'Life isn't fair, I need to control what people think of me.' Help the young person find examples of when these things aren't true and provide them with examples of the more helpful beliefs above.

Bibliotherapy

'You can learn from others.'

✓ Do you inspire and educate the young person through sharing examples of 'flawed protagonists'? Examples of literary characters or real-life people who have overcome challenge are really helpful for young people to learn from. Books, films and the internet are excellent sources of such role models. Examples include fictional characters like Frodo Baggins (*Lord of the Rings*), Forrest Gump, Hermione Granger (*Harry Potter*) and Katniss Everdeen (*Hunger Games*), or real people like Richard Branson, Oprah Winfrey, J.K. Rowling and Michael Jordan.

✓ Talk about characters in film and on TV; what do the young people think of them? What can they learn from them? Notice optimism in what you watch together and explicitly comment on this. We tend to get more of what we focus on.

✓ Is there anyone in your community, family or friendship group who could be used as a source of inspiration for the young person in terms of helpful attitudes, beliefs, values or behaviours to learn from? This person could provide a talk to the school, run an informal 'project' with the young person, act as a 'mentor' or become a 'pen pal'.

C-strategies

Communication

'You share your thoughts and feelings.'

✓ Does the young person have the skills and experience to communicate their needs effectively and appropriately? Or do they keep things bottled up? Give them opportunities to share their experiences daily in a no-pressure environment. Start small ('How was your day?') and build up to talking in more depth about how they felt about things. Some young people may prefer to do this through non-verbal means, e.g. writing things down or making artwork to reflect their inner world. All are valid and important methods of communicating what is going on for them. Show them that you value and respect their communication, whatever form it takes. Give them the space and opportunity to share this with you at whatever level they feel comfortable. Follow up on anything you find concerning; it may be a clue that the young person is asking for help.

✓ Do you model how to express yourself? We want our young people to see us communicating well with a range of people; friends, family, colleagues, members of the community, people in positions of authority, etc. It is also helpful for them to see us express ourselves through the things we choose to do, e.g. artwork, singing, dance, exercise, housework, amateur dramatics, etc! We want to share the message that it is okay to share all the different parts of yourself; you do not need to keep anything hidden away. It is important that young people know how to do this safely; they will learn lots from watching you.

Challenge

'You take risks to help yourself grow.'

✓ Does the young person feel able to take small and bigger risks, and to be creative? Or do they stay in their 'comfort zone'? Provide them with opportunities to do things differently and try new things, with your support. Praise moments of creativity and 'thinking outside the box'.

✓ Does the young person see you trying new things and taking risks, making yourself vulnerable by learning something unfamiliar and facing making mistakes? For example, this might be trying out a new piece of technology, taking a distance learning course, raising a concern with a neighbour, or attempting to fix something. They will learn a lot from seeing these behaviours modelled.

✓ Challenges can often be easier when attempted with someone else or in a group. Try new things as a class or family so that the focus is not entirely on the young person. Consider activities in which the young person may connect with a part not typically their area of focus or expertise. For example, some students high in perfectionism take great pleasure in activities involving animal care or crafts. Others may flourish in an activity involving playing with younger children or supporting the elderly.

✓ Challenge can also be easier away from familiar people who have come to know the young person in a certain way. Consider providing opportunities for the young person to try things away from their usual peer group or family group. These experiences can give the young person chance to try out 'being' a different way.

Coping

'You can get through difficult times.'

✓ Does the young person have the skills to cope with stress, such as relaxation techniques, and a social support network? Notice what the young person does during challenging times or when out of their comfort zone. Consider what you might prefer them to do instead.

✓ Teach the young person how to calm themselves down when their emotions are getting out of control. 'Emotion coaching' is a helpful approach; details about this can be found online.[2] Again, modelling your own emotion regulation is a powerful tool from which the young person can learn.

✓ Help the young person think about who they could talk to when things are getting difficult. You may need to help them build trusting relationships with people you think will be helpful in times of challenge.

✓ Support the young person to reflect on their skills; tune them into times when they solve problems or make choices (no matter how small) and help them reflect on these when things are getting hard.

✓ Consider the available 'role models' for the young person; whenever celebrities have taken their own lives, there is sadly an associated rise in suicide amongst young people. Children of parents who have taken their own lives are at much greater risk of also completing suicide. We learn ways to cope with life's pressures from those we identify with. Whenever you are aware of a TV, film or book character, or real person having 'coped' with their stresses in unhealthy ways (particularly through suicide), ensure you provide space for the young person to talk about this and at the very least provide an alternative narrative for them that reinforces the message that there are always other options, and to let someone know they are suffering or feeling hopeless so that they can help.

Compassion

'You are kind to yourself and others.'

✓ Does the young person show compassion to themselves? To other people? Do they treat themselves with the same care and consideration that they would a young child? Compassion is the opposite of criticism; it shows care, consideration and realistic expectations. Show this is important by modelling it and rewarding it where you notice it.

✓ Be compassionate to the young person, even when they are struggling to behave in ways you would like, 'pushing your buttons' or showing a lack of compassion to themselves. Compassion means wanting the best for the young person and helping them to help themselves. It sometimes means tolerating your own discomfort in the moment so that you can meet their needs.

✓ Be a positive role model for making mistakes and being kind to yourself about it. Notice if you are tense due to feeling under pressure or as though you are not getting something right. Explicitly comment on this in a kind and nurturing way, as though you were talking to a much younger version of yourself. Give yourself permission to laugh about it, in a compassionate rather than mocking way! Young people will pick up on this.

Choice

'You have control over what happens to you.'

✓ Does the young person have sufficient choice and control over what is happening in their life? What areas of their life do they truly have free choice in? Where young people experience a lack of choice and control in their life, they can become stressed, leading to seeking control over things like eating, their appearance and schoolwork. Can you provide them with more choices and therefore a greater sense of control? This can be over seemingly small and insignificant things at first, but they may make a big difference for the young person. Help them notice that their choices do not result in disaster, but help them get on in life.

✓ Does the young person perceive they have **too much** choice? This can be overwhelming. Sometimes young people need support to know how to make choices and prioritise. Help them find ways to make big decisions feel more manageable by breaking them down into smaller steps, writing pros and cons, seeking advice from trusted others, making a visual timetable, writing lists and Mind Maps, etc. Often choices are difficult to make because there is a fear over 'making the wrong one'. Help the young person plan for all eventualities so whatever happens with the decision they make, they will be okay. Make sure adults have the adult responsibilities and allow the young person the freedom to 'be a child'.

Further support

Table 7.2: Adults' 'quick-guide' summary of support

Spot unhelpful cognitions	Look out for students using 'should', 'must' or 'need' statements about what they're doing and explore these with them sensitively (e.g. Why should you? What could happen if you didn't? Why would that be bad? What other options are available to you?).
Reality check	Help students examine the evidence and test their hypotheses in 'safe' behaviour experiments (let's try...why don't you have a go...you could...check what happens if...).
Education	Teach them about perfectionism and optimalism and the link between their thoughts, feelings and behaviours.
Shift perspective	Consistently reinforce moving from an outcome- to a process-focused approach and away from comparing themselves with others. Develop their enjoyment for 'the moment' over achievement and outcome.
Skills development	Work on building their skills in compromising, prioritising, seeing the bigger picture and tolerating uncertainty, distress, discomfort and ambiguity through mindfulness and acceptance-based approaches.

The ideas below have been influenced by the Oxford High School for Girls 'Goodbye Little Miss Perfect' whole-school campaign.

Whole-school approach ideas
Introduction

- assembly for students to 'launch the campaign'

- talk with parents to answer any queries or concerns and to share the ideas

- use of optimalist signs around school (e.g. 'I can't do it...yet', 'It is good enough and I am good enough', pictures of different areas of life and balanced living, etc.).

Activities

- Visiting lecturers (e.g. from Higher Education) to teach the dangers of striving for perfection; the further you go in academia, there is less likely to be an answer that can be verified as correct or perfect; there is a need for creativity, self-belief and risk-taking.

- Use and reinforce positive self-talk to develop a shared language, e.g:

  - 'It's good enough.'

  - 'Let it go.'

  - 'Nobody's perfect.'

  - 'Have a go.'

- Help students think long term and see the bigger picture; the grades they get will be a springboard to their next steps, but in five years' time, no one will care what grades they got. Ex-students could come back and talk about what has happened since they left school: good and bad and how they coped.

- Use art, drama, music, dance and creative writing activities to express and explore feelings.

- Keep achievement logs to record all the non-academic things that have been achieved every day.

- Regularly discuss areas of life other than academia, e.g. What makes a good friend? How do you deal with anger? What do you do to relax?

- Ban mobile phones and encourage 'living in the moment'.

- Share stories and news reports of people who have still been successful and are liked despite making mistakes. Explore students' understanding of what qualities of a person are fixed and what can be changed.

- Compare famous people who have achieved success either through perfectionism or optimalism; reflect on their mental health and overall happiness with their lives. Consider ways in which some people are able to create a balance between success and happiness.

- Target/challenge each other to make a mistake in something important to them, and reflect on what happens next.

- Practise giving and receiving feedback by writing and giving each other complimentary notes.

- Build social skills and a sense of relatedness in projects involving the community, particularly 'vulnerable' members such as the elderly, disabled or young children.

- Encourage everyone to learn one new skill and keep a journal of their progress; reflect on this regularly with a trusted adult.

- Invite in visitors to introduce a new activity, something students are unlikely to have seen or tried before. Reflect on how much progress can be made and how much fun can be had when we try something new. Perhaps students could lead sessions teaching their peers or younger students something they enjoy doing as a hobby or something they feel good at.

- Increase emotional literacy teaching within school. An example particularly relevant to perfectionism is a demonstration in which a bottle of fizzy pop is shaken up repeatedly and then opened either all at once (messy and uncontrolled) or a little at a time (safe and controlled). Use this as a metaphor for expressing our emotions regularly rather than letting them all 'bottle up'. The same message can be conveyed through releasing air from a blown-up balloon either all at once by letting go (unpredictable and likely to go out of control) or a little at a time by keeping hold of the end (stays manageable).

- A healthy level of exercise is an excellent way to reduce mental health problems such as stress, anxiety and depression. Encourage a healthy attitude to exercise through whole-school daily routines such as a morning walk or lunchtime yoga.

- Whole-school relaxation sessions could also be introduced in which students are taught different ways to relax and unwind. These can be used as an opportunity to reflect on individual differences, preferences and needs, as everyone (adults as well as young people) will respond better to some calming strategies than others. Examples to try include:

  - being active, e.g. going for a walk, doing a puzzle, doodling...

- sharing your emotions, e.g. talking with someone about your feelings, writing in a journal, drawing/painting...

- using your senses, e.g. squeezing a cushion, smelling essential oil, looking at a calming photograph or image, listening to music, sipping a cup of tea...

- visualisation, e.g. imagining a calming place in detail, imagining yourself coping with a particular situation, remembering a pleasant experience...

- using your thoughts, e.g. repeating a mantra, practising positive self-talk, learning a motivational quote...

- relating to others, e.g. chatting with someone, watching others, offering help to others...

• Encourage groupwork sessions in which students research definitions of perfectionism amongst the school community and online, and discuss their own ideas. This can be used as an opportunity to explore the idea that some questions have no definite or 'right' answer, and the need for compromise. Consider times of dilemma when there is no 'solution', only a 'resolution'. Explore also the costs and perceived benefits of perfectionism and introduce the idea of optimalism as a positive opposite. Students could perhaps design their own posters or presentations to promote optimalism in school.

Plenary

• Organise student presentations on what they have **learnt** vs what they already **knew**. Encourage reflections on the emotional experience of learning, the power of mistakes and pride, and the sense of real achievement after effort and challenge.

- Share artwork/drama/dance/creative writing pieces with the rest of school and parents to celebrate what has been learnt and overcome relating to perfectionism.

- Plan for how to continue the optimalism over time; include short- and long-term targets and how this will be achieved.

Ongoing considerations

Remember to review the young person's progress over time and take the opportunity to celebrate their efforts and use of skills! Remember also to congratulate yourself for your own efforts in helping to change their behaviour.

- What progress is the student making towards their skill targets?

- Does anything need to be changed about the approach? If so, what and how?

- Are any other students now showing any concerning signs given our increased awareness and experience?

- What have we learned as professionals and parents and how could we use this in future to benefit students and our own children?

- **How will we celebrate progress?**

Endnotes

1 https://www.drdansiegel.com/resources/healthy_mind_platter

2 https://www.emotioncoachinguk.com/what-is-emotion-coaching

Chapter 8

Strategies for Young People

'Change can be hard, but possible, and worth it.'

Ready...

This chapter is specifically for young people who feel they are high in perfectionism and would like some ideas about how to move away from perfectionist ways of thinking and behaving and move closer towards an 'optimalist' lifestyle.

Optimalism is a way of thinking, feeling and behaving that is more likely than perfectionism to result in success **and** happiness. The strategies to help you get there are set out as 'ABCs' to make them easier to read and remember. There is also a table of 'optimalist' goals at the end of the chapter for you to work towards.

Set...

I thoroughly recommend an 'optimalist' approach to these strategies:

- ✓ You do not have to remember or try all these things.

- ✓ Even if you just try out one or two that will be a positive move in the right direction.

- ✓ It is better to try, even if you feel unsuccessful, than not to try at all. Making mistakes is an important part of learning and even though they may feel unpleasant, you can take something from the experience to make things even better next time.

✓ Start small and work up.

✓ Ask for help in a way in which you feel comfortable to do so.

✓ Remember, change is possible with time, practice and opportunity.

✓ If you change nothing else, try saying this to yourself regularly until it becomes a fixed belief:

'I am good enough.'

You might not believe it *yet*, but with enough repetition, one day you will.

Go!

The ABCs are shown in Table 8.1 and explained in more detail over the following pages.

Table 8.1: The 'ABCs' of challenging perfectionism

A	B	C
Acceptance	Balance	Communication
Attention	Boundaries	Challenge
Advice	Behaviour	Coping
Attitude	Beliefs	Compassion
Assertiveness	Bibliotherapy	Choice

A-strategies

Acceptance

'I am enough.'

✓ Tell yourself: 'I will *always* have strengths *and* difficulties because I am human.' Let this become your mantra. Write it on a note and stick it somewhere you can read it daily. One day you will internalise it and it will become your inner voice.

✓ Draw a stick person in the middle of the page. This is you. On one half of the page write down all your strengths (ask others to help if needed). On the other half write down all the things you find difficult or dislike about yourself and would like to change or be better at. This is a visual way to see yourself as balanced, not all one thing or another. A healthy mixture! A human.

✓ Draw/list the qualities of your ideal self on one side of a page and your non-ideal self on the other. Draw a line between the two to make a scale. Where are you now on this scale? What little steps could you take to be more like your ideal self? Is your 'ideal self' realistic and achievable? If not, change the words you use to describe it. Self-esteem comes from accepting who you are.

✓ Draw a suitcase and inside write all the things that are valuable to you. What is important to **you**? Stick on or draw pictures to reflect your values and look at this often. These are your personal values and are important to remember. Are you living your life according to these values, or someone else's? The more you are true to your values, the more at peace you will feel with yourself.

✓ Learn more about perfectionism and optimalism in books and online. You will find there are lots of people like you who might have helpful tips. Read biographies of people who have achieved despite adversity, and you will move closer to accepting yourself exactly as you are. Flaws and all! 'Difficulties', 'differences' and 'deficits' you may come across include people who have experienced loss, injury, or trauma; those with diagnosable physical or mental ill health; individuals from very challenging backgrounds or in difficult current living conditions; those who have made a series of mistakes, or perhaps one life-changing mistake; men and women who have succeeded despite previous rejection and 'failure'; young people who have achieved greatness in spite of their age and barriers in their way. Examples to get you started include: Greta Thunberg, J.K. Rowling, Colonel Sanders, Albert Einstein, Walt Disney, Richard Branson, Steven Spielberg, the Beatles, Michael Jordan, and Thomas Edison. There are lots more; find someone who appeals to you and explore their story. Can you find any similarities with your own? What can you learn from their journey?

✓ Accept that this is how you are **now**, but you **can** change! Both are possible. Both are okay. For example, it is okay that you like things to be perfect, and yet you are also able to become more able to accept 'good enough'. You may get very upset over mistakes now, and that is fine! However you can also become more tolerant of these over time. It is okay for you to be a bit of a worrier, and to know that you can become more relaxed as you get older. Accepting who you are now **and** acknowledging you can change in the future are both possible, okay and helpful. The two ideas help us feel validated (as though our feelings are true and worthwhile) **and** provide motivation and hope for our future.

Attention

'I am important.'

✓ Everyone needs attention in some way. Think about who in your life gives you the kind of attention that makes you feel genuinely good about yourself. Perhaps they focus on the areas of most value to you, perhaps they fully accept you as you are, perhaps they are interested in how you feel. Can you spend more time with these people? Sometimes we avoid these people as we are more used to trying to gain the attention of people 'less available' to us. An idea to remind you to focus your attention on the people who give you positive attention is to add an icon next to their name in your phone (e.g. an apple to signify health, growth, and nurture), then whenever they send you a message or you scroll through your contact list you will be reminded to redirect your attention to them rather than avoid them.

✓ Look online to find Dr Daniel Siegel's 'Healthy Mind Platter'. Use this image to think about balancing out the attention you give to your daily activities: sleep (necessary for consolidation of the day's learning and for the body to recover from its experiences); physical activity (movement to strengthen the body and mind); connecting with others and the natural world (instead of being in front of a screen); reflection (focusing on your inner world of sensations, thoughts and feelings); play (being free, spontaneous and creative to allow the brain to make new connections); focus (having mindful concentration on a task to make deep connections in the brain); and downtime (opportunity for your mind to wander without any specific goals to help the brain recharge). Work towards achieving a balance, or at the very least not neglecting or overdoing any areas. Perhaps print out an image of this and stick it somewhere you will notice it daily; this can be a helpful reminder to balance our activities.

Advice

'I seek help when I need it.'

✓ What are the areas you find more challenging? Or areas you enjoy or are good at but would like to improve further? Think about who you could ask to help guide you with these things. Consider who would make a helpful 'mentor' or 'coach', someone who will not be critical but instead guide you step by step along the journey to improvement. This can be a book or internet video if you do not yet feel comfortable asking someone for help.

✓ 'We all need help sometimes.' Remind yourself of this often and allow it to become your inner voice. Your 'optimalist' attitude will remind you that we all have the potential to grow and improve, and that often we need some form of advice and guidance to help us do this. 'It is perfectly okay to ask for help.' In fact, this is often the wise thing to do.

Attitude

'I have a growth mindset.'

✓ Tell yourself: 'Good enough is perfectly okay!' Repeat this often. Store it on your phone, write it on a sticky note on your academic planner, make a poster of it for your wall... Messages we repeat daily can quickly become ingrained in our minds as automatic thoughts.

✓ Notice your thoughts over the course of a week. Write your 'all-or-nothing' thoughts on two sides of a see-saw. What would be a fair middle-ground? Try this for all your 'black-or-white' thinking. Life is full of compromises and it takes practice to see these.

✓ Move on to the next thing by distracting yourself with activity. This can be something physical (like going for a mindful walk or run, or sorting out your clothes or bookshelves), something sensory (like stroking a pet, having a hot shower or looking through uplifting images), something mundane and repetitive (like doing the washing-up, or tidying or organising your belongings) or something more cerebral or creative (like a sudoku puzzle, wordsearch, reading a book or magazine, or doodling). If you start to dwell on what you've done, repeat 'Good enough is perfectly okay' and get active. Your mind is stuck on a loop – they are thoughts but they are not facts. Use activity to calm and distract your brain from repetitive thoughts.

✓ Practise compromising and notice how much more you can achieve. You will need to begin to tolerate the uncomfortable feeling; it will get less over time as you get 'stronger' at tolerating discomfort without trying to push it away. For example, if you have a tendency to dwell on things you have done, notice when you are doing this, tell yourself 'I am going to put these thoughts aside and get on' and involve yourself in something else. When you notice feelings of tension, worry or stress (these are likely as your brain is used to you going over the same thoughts rather than moving away from them), use coping skills until these feelings are reduced enough to allow you to get on with something else. Ways to cope with the discomfort include mindful breathing (such as counting to ten while gently breathing in and out and noticing the feeling of this in your chest and throat), visualisation (carefully picturing a pleasing scene in detail, using all your senses in your imagination) or progressive muscle relaxation (squeezing then releasing each muscle in your body in turn from your toes up to your head).

✓ Look up Human Rights. Ask people what they think 'Rights and Responsibilities' are. These are the really important things in life! For all other things, it is okay to not always achieve the highest standard.

✓ Get some perspective by reading about people much less fortunate than you; for example, those living in war-torn countries, people sleeping rough (homeless), or those without easy access to healthcare or education. You could perhaps find ways to give your time and energy to help those more vulnerable than you. Make a list of what things are **really** important in life and what things only **seem** important at the time. Refer to this often.

✓ Read about 'growth mindset' and start to give yourself helpful messages: 'I can change, I can grow, I can learn' and 'Mistakes and emotions are a valuable and necessary part of being human.' Notice who in your life, or perhaps on TV, in films or in books, also has this attitude. Make them your new role model.

✓ Write yourself a mantra on a note you can see every day. This mantra could be 'Learn to fail or fail to learn.' This will serve as a reminder that mistakes are part of learning and developing.

Another mantra could be 'There is no real success if there was never a chance of failure.' Authentic pride comes from genuine achievement.

Assertiveness

'I can get my needs met without upsetting anyone.'

✓ Can you express your thoughts and feelings to a range of people without becoming upset or upsetting them? Can you get your needs met? If these things provoke anxiety or result in relationship problems, you could work on developing your assertiveness skills. Tell yourself two important messages:

- my thoughts, feelings, wants, needs and beliefs are important

- other people's thoughts, feelings, wants, needs and beliefs are important.

✓ Practise a 'script' to help you share important messages without becoming upset. The more you practise it, the easier it will be to say to the person involved.

✓ Tell yourself 'It is okay to say 'no'. 'No' can be a complete sentence. You do not need to justify your response. You could practise this in advance, including how you will manage the feelings it provokes.

✓ Apologise when you have done something to upset someone. Take responsibility for your actions (but only your actions; you are not responsible for other people's feelings, thoughts or behaviours).

B-strategies

Balance

'I spend my time and effort on different areas of my life.'

✓ Tell yourself: 'Other areas of my life are important too.' Remind yourself of this often.

✓ Draw a pie chart and split it into six sections to show how much time and effort you spend on the following areas of your life: school/work, health, relationships, daily living (cleanliness, travel, chores, etc.), recreation (hobbies/leisure), spirituality (having a purpose, e.g. helping others). How does this differ from a pie chart with all sections equal? This should show which areas you can give more attention and which you can give less.

✓ Write down the pros and cons (short term and long term) of giving your time and energy to your area of value and neglecting the others. Does this shift your thinking slightly?

Boundaries

'I set myself reasonable limits.'

✓ Tell yourself: 'First I am going to...then I will...' This helps give a structure to our activities.

✓ Ask yourself: 'What is the *purpose* of this task?' 'What is reasonable?' 'What is the priority?' 'What exactly do I need to achieve here?' Stop during the task and ask yourself these questions again. Pull yourself back from doing more than what is needed.

✓ Make a timetable or list of all the things you want/need to do. Write down how long you will spend on them. Then break down each task into small steps and tick them off as you go. Check the time and list as you go – you may need to change your plan if it becomes clear you have planned too much to fit in. Don't be self-critical if this is the case! Planning realistically is a skill – you will get better at planning a reasonable amount of work for yourself the more you practise!

✓ Consider/note down your boundaries in other areas of your life (physical, emotional, social) – what are you willing to accept and tolerate and what is too much? Boundaries help us navigate our way through life safely and successfully. There are guides online to help you stay healthy and safe.[1]

✓ Work **smart** not **hard**. Make efficient use of your time by noting how long you are spending on things and considering how you can 'cut corners' yet still get the task done. Ask people who seem to make good use of their time for tips.

Behaviour

'I do things to challenge myself.'

✓ Tell yourself: 'The way I behave will change how I think and feel.' Remind yourself of this often.

✓ Try out a behaviour experiment: think of something that makes you a bit worried (e.g. knocking something over in a shop, disagreeing with someone, creasing the corner of your work, etc) and do it! Notice what happens and tell yourself: 'It's okay.' Notice the anxiety go down on its own as you repeat this to yourself. Reflect on your successful experiment! Often our 'worst-case scenario' either does not happen or is not that bad after all. This can change the way we think to make our ideas and beliefs more helpful for us. If you feel unable to tackle this alone, seek the support of an appropriate adult who can help you take on this challenge.

✓ Don't always trust your anxiety. It can keep you trapped in a vicious cycle. The best way to overcome anxiety is to 'feel the fear and do it anyway'. The actual thing we fear is often less frightening than the idea we built up in our mind. Our imagination is usually far worse than reality. Don't just take my word for it, try it out for yourself!

✓ There is no real success if there was never a chance of failure. When we limit ourselves to only doing things we **know** we will be good at, we will never feel a deep sense of pride or achievement. Nor will we grow as people. Try out something you do not feel so confident in achieving; when you put in effort to develop your skills to achieve this and eventually overcome the challenge, the sense of pride will be immense and you will have grown as a person.

Beliefs

'I believe in myself.'

✓ What do you believe about yourself, your abilities, your personality, etc? These are likely to be 'automatic thoughts' that pop up, especially when you are put under pressure. Try to notice them and write them down. This brings them out into the open so you can look at them and start working to change them if they are unkind or unhelpful.

✓ Try to write down a helpful and kind belief for every belief you record that is unhelpful. Practise telling yourself this new version whenever you hear yourself say the original. Over time, you can change the way you think through practice. 'Fake it 'til you make it!' Our brains can and do change with repeated practice.

✓ What do you believe about other people, about their abilities and what you can expect from them? Again, notice any automatic thoughts you have about other people and again challenge these with alternative beliefs. Practise, practise, practise.

✓ Write down your new, helpful thoughts somewhere you can see them daily. This will remind you to practise telling them to yourself. Examples include:

- 'I am okay.'

- 'I can do this.'

- 'They are trying their best.'

- 'They could be helpful if I give them a chance.'

Bibliotherapy

'I can learn from others.'

✓ You are not expected to figure this all out yourself. Life is big and full of challenges, and there are people you can learn from who have 'been there and done that'. Look online or in books for people who have been through challenge and how they have overcome this to achieve. Famous autobiographies and memoirs you could try include those of Benjamin Franklin, Maya Angelou, Nelson Mandela, Andre Agassi and Phil Knight. There may be members of your community or family who are inspiring in their own way; take a lesson from these people and speak with them if you feel comfortable to do so. How do others cope with their challenges? Learn from them. Try out these skills for yourself. Develop your own 'armoury' of coping skills for when times get tough.

✓ Get book and film recommendations from others. You may find some surprising and inspiring stories that stick with you and become an important part of shaping your character!

✓ When you find someone you find inspiring, stick their picture somewhere you will see it regularly and use it as a reminder of the kinds of attitudes, beliefs, values and behaviours you would like to model yourself. Perhaps write down words that represent these qualities on the picture as an extra reminder.

C-strategies

Communication

'I share my thoughts and feelings.'

✓ Tell yourself: 'My thoughts and feelings are important to share.' Emotions are designed to flow freely and help inform us about what we need. They are not meant to be shut away. By suppressing our emotions, they just build up energy and eventually burst out of us in uncontrolled ways. They need airing and freedom. Let them out!

✓ Ask yourself: 'How am I feeling?'; 'What am I thinking?' Learn to become aware of your thoughts and feelings.

✓ Keep a daily journal: record your thoughts and feelings from the day in a way that appeals to you (e.g. words, song lyrics, famous quotes, pictures, photographs...).

✓ Improve your emotional vocabulary – write down as many feeling words as you can **and** their opposites. Try to visualise a time you have felt like these (or seen someone feeling like this). Add to the list over time and try to fill in words between the two opposites to build up a 'continuum' of emotions. Look up a list of emotion words on the internet; think about what each one might feel like and when you might have experienced it in your life so far.

✓ Use art materials to express your thoughts and feelings on paper/canvas (the aim is to **express,** not create a work of art! The 'finished product' can be stored somewhere privately, recycled or thrown away if you prefer! Or use it to inspire an actual piece of artwork).

✓ Dance or sing to your favourite tune somewhere you can be alone, as loudly and dramatically as possible! Watch a film that really speaks to you; it is likely it is helping you process some deep feelings.

✓ Make a list or draw a picture of all the people in your life you could talk to. Some people you would prefer to have fun with, and others you can be more serious with. Be clear which is which.

✓ Start to observe different people's communication style: is it passive, aggressive, passive-aggressive, or assertive? Copy the style of the assertive people (look up these terms if you are unsure).

✓ Practise expressing yourself by writing a letter to someone about any 'unsaid' things – destroy it when finished or consider sending if appropriate and you are prepared to deal with any consequences.

Challenge

'I take risks to help myself grow.'

✓ Tell yourself: 'I can do it'; 'This will be an adventure'; 'It will be worth the risk in the end.' Repeat these things often.

✓ Try something new, this can be anything! From putting your socks on in a different order, to sitting in a different chair in the dining room, to taking a different route to school. Notice that although it feels different, it is okay! Build up to bigger steps, like handing in work having only read it through once, or talking to someone new at breaktime. The more challenges you take, the bigger your comfort zone will grow! Just imagine what you could achieve in your life! There is a very helpful saying here: 'feel the fear and do it anyway'. Don't always trust your fear – sometimes it will hold you back. Another helpful saying is 'there is no real success if there was no chance of failure'. Challenge yourself and **grow**!

Coping

'I can get through difficult times.'

✓ Tell yourself: 'I can cope.' Write this on a note you look at regularly.

✓ Try out the following 'multi-modal' coping skills to find out your personal coping style; which work best for you to help release your tension?

- **Behaviour** (do something, e.g. go for a walk, do a puzzle...).

- **Affect** (talk about your feelings, write in journal, paint, watch a film...).

- **Senses** (squeeze a toy, smell an essential oil, look at a comforting photograph, listen to music, have a cup of tea...).

- **Imagery** (picture a calming place in detail, picture yourself coping...).

- **Cognition** (positive self-talk, repeat a mantra, e.g. 'it's okay'...).

- **Interpersonal** (seek out company, chat with someone, offer help...).

- **Drugs/biology** (cut down caffeine, try exercise, see your family doctor...).

✓ Draw a toolbox or bag and inside write all the different 'tools' and tricks you have that you can use when getting stressed. Keep it somewhere you can find it when needed.

✓ Remember – feeling stressed sometimes is normal! Everyone must learn to cope. Anxiety makes our 'thinking' brain shut down; coping skills help it work again.

✓ Practise mindfulness as a helpful coping strategy. Consider the following visualisation as a way to start:

- **Imagine the sky.** This is a metaphor for your mind and your true self. No matter what is going on in the sky, it is always there. Present, stable, consistent. All around you. You are always present, like the sky.

- **Imagine the clouds.** These are a metaphor for your thoughts. Clouds come and go, floating past into and out of our awareness. Thoughts too are not permanent. Allow the clouds in your visualisation to float out of awareness; imagine any thoughts floating away with them. Thoughts, like clouds, vary in size, shape and intensity.

- **Imagine the weather.** This is a metaphor for your emotions. The weather changes and can range from gentle and serene to raw and powerful. It can feel pleasurable, neutral, dreary or frightening. Notice how the weather changes and so too does your mood. Allow your visualisation to match your current emotional state. Notice how you can gently change the weather in your visualisation to help change your current mood.

- **Imagine birds, planes, hot air balloons, leaves or anything else you can visualise floating, flying or soaring in the air.** These can be metaphors for things that are happening in your life: people, places, experiences. Notice how they are moving, what attention you are paying them and where they might be going.

- **Notice how the sky is still present and stable no matter what is happening in it.** Keep bringing your awareness back to the current moment and remind yourself that you are stable and okay.

Compassion

'I am kind to myself and others.'

✓ Tell yourself: 'It's okay'; 'Never mind' and 'Let's have another go.' Repeat these often.

✓ Ask yourself: 'What is the purpose of this task?'; 'What is really important in this?'; 'What is the most effective way to achieve that?', whenever you notice self-critical thoughts about what you 'should be' doing.

✓ Ask your teacher/friend/parent what approach they would take and try it out to see if it works for you; school years are for experimenting with how you learn best so try out some different approaches that are less exhausting than what you currently do.

✓ To reduce worrying, ask yourself 'Is this a problem I can solve?' – if so, use calming strategies to get your brain in the right state to think, then note down all the possible ways to solve the problem. Choose one and go for it. If it doesn't work, you know to try something else next time. If it's not a problem you can solve, there's nothing you can do about it so there is no use worrying about it! Find something to distract yourself. Don't trust the worry! It is like a rocking chair: it gives us something to do but doesn't get us very far.

✓ Reward yourself when you **do** achieve something, no matter how small. Record your progress and achievements in a 'positives book/folder' and treat yourself often. Life is for living!

✓ Notice when you think/say 'should' or 'need' and replace with kinder words like 'could' and 'would prefer'.

Choice

'I have control over what happens to me.'

✓ We can become stressed if we do not feel we have control or choice in our lives. Think about what choices you do have in your life, even if they seem very small, like what clothes you put on in the morning, how you style your hair or what music you listen to or book you choose to read. Making decisions about the little things will help build your confidence to make decisions about the bigger things. Notice that you can make choices and things generally work out okay!

✓ We may also feel overwhelmed if it feels as though we have too much choice or responsibility and cannot make a decision. At times like this, write a list, draw a timetable or image of what is going on, make a list of pros and cons, or seek advice from someone you trust. Often there is no 'right answer' or solution to a problem situation, only a *resolution*. This means there will be pros and cons of the choice you make, but that is okay and reflects the real world. Learn to tolerate these decisions and to focus on moving forwards with your choice rather than dwelling on what you did not choose.

✓ Find out where to go for help if you need it. This can be people, like your family doctor, someone in school, a member of your community, someone on the end of a helpline, or a website which has guidance or online chat to support you. Knowing we have choice, even in difficult times, can help reduce our stress. **Remember, we always have a choice, even when it feels like we don't.**

Further support

Table 8.1 highlights the self-talk and activities to help move you towards more 'optimalist' thinking.

✓ Changing the way you talk to yourself will begin to change your thoughts.

✓ Changing your behaviours will also help to change your thoughts.

✓ Practise, practise, practise and these thoughts will become automatic.

✓ They will replace the perfectionist thoughts over time.

Table 8.1: Optimalism self-talk ideas

Optimalist thought	Self-talk to help achieve this	Activities to help achieve this
I see the journey as an irregular spiral	There are likely to be bumps along the way. I may have to stop, reflect and change my strategy. It is rare to get to a target in a smooth journey and this would be an unreasonable expectation.	Stop! Think about what you are doing. Is it getting you to where you want to go? If not, what can you do differently? Don't mindlessly plough on; this is a waste of time and effort! Look up ways of doing things online; there may be a quicker/better/smarter way.
I view failure as feedback	Mistakes are how we learn and succeed best. Everyone makes mistakes and they don't often end in disaster! What have I learned from my 'failure'? I am growing as a person. I am not what I do, I am me. I am human!	Make a mistake. Do it! Challenge your worst fear by confronting it head-on. Then think about what this has taught you. Experience will teach you that you can cope and learn something.

I focus on the journey and the destination	Life is mostly about what you do on your way to your destination. It is good to have an end to journey towards, but it is the journey that matters in the end. Enjoy the ride. Find pleasure in the small, everyday things and in interactions with others.	Try out some fun activities (games, sports, reading, cinema, painting...) and notice how much enjoyment and relaxation you can experience when you are 'in the moment', rather than worrying about the outcome, the next thing or what you've just done. Make connections with others rather than always focusing on the task. Set deadlines and reflect on these periodically to ensure they are still realistic and achievable.
My thinking is realistic and complex	There are lots of points between the extremes that may also be necessary and valuable. There may not be a 'solution', only a 'resolution'. I can tolerate the 'middle ground'.	Notice the thought and say it out loud. Does it sound extreme and dramatic? If so, try laughing at it. Find the 'middle ground', i.e. a compromise. Imagine you are helping a child – what would you say to them to stop them fretting? Making an action plan stops the anxiety in its tracks.
I am fair and balanced	I am no different from anyone else. We all have the same needs. I am no more or no less special. I am a human being. I notice when I need things.	Ask yourself what you would expect from a friend in this situation. You are worthy of these expectations too. The more you practise, the more this will feel true. Write down your rights and needs.
I am open to suggestions	I recognise the value of feedback. I can learn and improve from it, and will actively seek it and be grateful to those who give it constructively and purposefully. Feedback is about what I do, not who I am.	There's a fine line between seeking feedback and seeking reassurance and approval. Ask someone you trust once (and once only) for specific feedback. If you don't understand, ask them to be even more specific. You are aiming to learn about your strengths and needs, not seeking validation for you as a person. This cannot come from someone else.

cont.

Optimalist thought	Self-talk to help achieve this	Activities to help achieve this
I am a benefit finder	Look on the bright side; find the rainbow in the rain. But be realistic! No one likes someone who is always pessimistic or always optimistic. Try to notice the good things in the situation.	Write down three positives that have happened to/for you at the end of each day. Keep a 'jar of positives' and write down things that you have done that have been enjoyable and/or successful. Look through these at the end of each month.
I am forgiving	I take responsibility for my mistakes. I learn from my failures. I understand that making mistakes and experiencing failure are unavoidable. I am human. It is okay to be imperfect.	Spend some time with children or animals. Reflect on how you treat them. This is how you need to be treating yourself too – with compassion and warmth, not criticism and judgement. You have the same basic needs and will suffer if they are not met. Notice your critical thoughts and replace them with kinder ones.
I am adaptable and dynamic	I set ambitious goals but am not chained to these commitments. I have a clear sense of direction but am open to different alternatives. I am purposeful and open to possibilities. I stop and reflect on what I'm doing, changing my path if needed.	Try doing something different each day, no matter how small. Even doing your hair differently or sitting somewhere different at lunch can be enough to start 're-wiring' your brain. Prove to yourself that you can change and still be in control.

Good luck, enjoy the journey!

Endnote

1   https://psychcentral.com/lib/the-importance-of-personal-boundaries

Appendix A: My Research

My 2016 research was prompted by the lack of clarity in the existing literature over perfectionism, along with the lack of qualitative information of how the construct of 'perfectionism' is understood by young people themselves and the key adults in their lives.

My interpretative study had two parts; the first explored the perceptions of 32 students, parents and school staff in four high-achieving schools in England relating to perfectionism, success and happiness.

Key findings of this part of the research include:

- Participants believed perfectionism related to desired outcomes, particularly achievement. Perfectionism was associated with **positive behaviours** such as striving, conscientiousness and neatness. Only two participants were aware of the link between perfectionism, mental health problems and suicide. The main 'risks' perceived were relatively minor; for example, being an annoyance to others and missing out on leisure time.

- Participants believed that making mistakes was a bad thing and that making mistakes in the 'real world' could lead to serious consequences such as death or imprisonment. Someone who made mistakes was considered a failure and someone who could not be successful or happy.

- Participants identified that people high in perfectionism may not be happy or experience emotional wellbeing.

Perfectionism was associated with **negative thoughts and feelings** such as paranoia, torment, dread and misery.

- Participants believed that the opposite of a 'perfectionist' was someone they definitely would not want themselves/ their child/their student to be. This person was believed to be lazy, unsuccessful and disruptive. They were someone who made a lot of mistakes. Most participants would rather themselves/child/student were higher rather than lower in perfectionism.

- Participants linked achievement with happiness but realised that this association could not support their existing view of perfectionism. There was a conflict over the associations between perfectionism, success and emotional wellbeing, prompting a need for guidance and clarity.

- Participants felt that students high in perfectionism could change but would probably be conflicted about changing. There were very minimal suggestions of ways to help someone become 'less perfectionist'. Some participants felt that someone high in perfectionism could only change if something drastic happened to them. There was mixed opinion over whether it would be hard for individuals to change as there were conflicted opinions (even from the same participants) over whether perfectionism is something people are born with or something created through experiences and upbringing, including the impact of social media. Only one participant felt that someone high in perfectionism may struggle to see that there was a problem; no one identified that they may struggle to seek or receive help. A large majority of participants did not feel that someone high in perfectionism should change, unless there was an obvious detrimental effect on them.

- Participants largely believed that a 'non-perfectionist' is 'born that way' yet also felt it would be easy for them to become 'more perfectionist' than for someone high in perfectionism to become less so. One parent suggested that it should be 'non-perfectionists' we are trying to change so that they become more 'perfectionist'.

Therefore the major gaps in participant knowledge and understanding were as follows relating to someone high in perfectionism:

- at risk of not seeking help when needed

- at risk of mental health problems and even suicide

- at risk of underachievement or burnout, rather than consistent success

- at risk of social isolation and may require support to build social support networks

- may not be aware of their own 'perfectionist' thoughts and behaviours

- may go unnoticed

- may need particular help with stress management and increasing their sense of pride.

There was also a clear gap around schools and families being aware of the powerful role they have in either keeping unhelpful perfectionism patterns going or being able to challenge them to change into something healthier. A related notable gap in participant knowledge and understanding was the fact that early intervention can be helpful in preventing perfectionism; if people are not aware of this, or not aware of the markers for perfectionism, this is a considerable missing link in perfectionism intervention.

The second part of the research discussed the above findings with the following range of health and education professionals:

- Art Psychotherapist

- Child and Adolescent Psychiatrist

- Cognitive Behavioural Therapist

- Dialectical Behavioural Therapist/Mental Health Nurse

- Integrative Counsellor

- Lead Specialist Practitioner in Psychotherapy/Mental Health Nurse

- three Educational Psychologists.

The views of these professionals, combined with the existing research and psychological theory, shaped the strategies shared in this book.

Appendix B: Support Agencies Around the World

Please note, this is not an exhaustive list and there are considerably more UK support agencies noted than for the rest of the world due to my location of work. There may be similar support agencies in your particular region.

Region	Support Agencies	Websites
Australia	Australian Centre for Grief and Bereavement	www.grief.org.au
	Beyond Blue	www.beyondblue.org.au
	Hope Bereavement Care	www.bereavement.org.au
	Mental Health Australia	www.mhaustralia.org
	SANE Australia	www.sane.org
	Samaritans	www.thesamaritans.org.au
Canada	Your Health in Mind	www.yourhealthinmind.org
	HealthLinkBC	www.healthlinkbc.ca
	Various	www.canadianliving.com/health/mind-and-spirit/article/where-to-find-mental-health-support-in-canada
Ireland	Health Service Executive	www2.hse.ie/mental-health
	HSCNI Bereavement Network	www.hscbereavementnetwork.hscni.net/bereavement-care/bereavement-support-organisations
	Mental Health Ireland	www.mentalhealthireland.ie
	Samaritans	www.samaritans.org

cont.

Region	Support Agencies	Websites
New Zealand	A Memory Tree	www.amemorytree.co.nz
	Grief Centre	www.griefcentre.org.nz
	Mental Health Foundation of New Zealand	www.mentalhealth.org.nz
	Samaritans	www.samaritans.org.nz
	Supporting Families in Mental Illness	www.supportingfamilies.org.nz
UK	Cruse Bereavement Care	www.cruse.org.uk
	Mental Health Foundation	www.mentalhealth.org.uk
	Mental Health Helplines	www.nhs.uk/conditions/stress-anxiety-depression/mental-health-helplines
	Mental Health UK	www.mentalhealth-uk.org
	Mental Health Support	www.mentalhealthsupport.co.uk/organisations.html
	Mind	www.mind.org.uk
	Papyrus Prevention of Young Suicide	www.papyrus-uk.org
	Rethink	www.rethink.org
	Samaritans	www.samaritans.org
	Sane	www.sane.org.uk
	Sue Ryder Bereavement Support	www.sueryder.org
	Support After Suicide Partnership	www.supportaftersuicide.org.uk
	Time to Change	www.time-to-change.org.uk
	Winston's Wish	www.winstonswish.org
USA	Mental Health America	www.mentalhealthamerica.net
	Samaritans USA	www.samaritansusa.org
	Very Well Health	www.verywellhealth.com/grief-loss-bereavement-support-groups-1132533

Appendix C: Using Art Therapeutically

The theory

- Artistic expression has the power to help in healing through **resolving internal conflicts**, raising self-esteem and self-awareness through **self-expression and validation of internal experiences**, and simply providing **relaxation and relief of tension**.

- This creative and expressive outlet can improve physical and mental health and emotional wellbeing.

- It does not rely on language, as with most other forms of therapy, so unconscious processes relating to emotional pain can be effectively targeted in a way that is unavailable in more 'talking-based' therapies.

- Using art therapeutically requires **few materials** and **no artistic background**. Often, the less artistic you perceive yourself to be, the better.

- Therapeutic art activities are less about the final product and more about the **transformation that occurs along the way**.

What to do when using art therapeutically

✓ Allow freedom for any form of expression (no matter

how 'disturbing', confusing, complicated or simple). View the art as a place of emotional safety, exploration and experimentation.

✓ Be present; a trusted adult close by can often help a young person express more through art than if they were trying the activities alone.

✓ Show you value the young person's artistic (and related self-) expression by keeping their work safe (if they will allow you to do so).

What not to do when using art therapeutically

- Avoid making any 'value-judgements' about the art; it is not about how good/neat/pretty it looks, but rather the effort and engagement of the young person.

- Avoid interpreting the art (e.g. it looks like you're angry/ that person looks like…). These interpretations can be threatening, disempowering, inhibiting and just plain wrong!

- Avoid being rejecting, ridiculing or dismissive in any way about the art produced (e.g. the bin is a completely inappropriate place for you to put the artwork. The young person may choose to do this but must not see you as 'throwing away' their expression).

Example activities to try

- Keep an art journal by sketching an image to represent your day/key experience from your day.

- Make a 'self-soothe' book or box containing uplifting images.

- Draw repeating patterns over a page and colour in using just two or three colours.

- Print a famous painting and add your own ideas to it.

- Paint an uplifting design onto a stone and leave it somewhere to be found.

- Create a collage using cut-out pictures and text from magazines/newspapers/old greetings cards.

- Try out 'dark drawing' – draw without looking then see what you've created once finished.

- Weave or tie together scraps of fabric and hang them from a tree branch to represent feelings, memories or wishes.

- Doodle squiggly lines using a pen or pencil and not taking it off the page; fill in the spaces to make different characters or scenes.

- Make your own dream catcher to hang over your bed at night.

- Take an old item of clothing, soft toy or broken household object and recycle it into something new.

- Make a vision board by sticking images together to inspire and motivate you towards your goals.

- Build a shrine to someone you love or admire – include anything you choose.

- Design a postcard – send it if you choose.

- Paint an image onto a window to be seen from both sides.

- Make your own mark-making tool from anything you can find and use it to make an image.

- Create an image using paints and your body – no mark-making tools.

- Use watercolour paints to colour-in a body shape on paper – match colours, shapes and intensity to how you feel in different parts of your body.

- Draw a picture using your non-dominant hand.

- Make a temporary sculpture using fruit, vegetables or other items found in nature.

- Make a mask to pretend to be someone else, e.g. more powerful, daring, etc. It can be as simple as a cut-out piece of paper, or more elaborate like papier-mache. Stick things on to make it more three-dimensional.

- Create little characters with clay or playdough to represent your biggest strengths and fears.

- Build a den and make it feel personal and safe inside.

- Draw on the floor or wall outside using chunky wax crayons or chalk.

- Choose an object that appeals to you and use it as a stencil to create a pattern.

Note: This list of activities has been adapted from huffingtonpost.com.

Appendix D: Oxford High School GDST (Girls' Day School Trust) Whole-School Project to Challenge Unhelpful Perfectionism

School newsletter article reflecting on the approach (Dr Sarah Squire, Deputy Head – Students and Staff 2013–2019)

GOODBYE LITTLE MISS PERFECT!

During the last two weeks of June, Oxford High School waved goodbye to Little Miss Perfect! Some of her behaviours had become quite unhelpful; she was known to put off starting a piece of work because she didn't feel confident about being able to do it 'perfectly', consider herself a 'failure' if her friend achieved a higher mark and spend ages on beautifully written notes (ripping out the page if she made an error which might make the presentation less than perfect). Instead, Oxford High School focused on enhancing attainment and well being, by encouraging girls not to be held back by perfectionism, because our students need to understand and value the importance of welcoming error in the process of rigorous learning. We want them to experience the complex, the unfamiliar, and the 'not yet'. As one of the Year 7 girls explained (in French!) to Madame Parfaite, 'You are annoying because you have nothing to learn.'

We were delighted that Professor Roz Shafran gave the annual Ada Benson lecture on 'Perfectionism and self-esteem: two sides of the same coin?' She explained the difference between a girl having high standards (obviously to be encouraged) and a girl's self-esteem being disproportionately dependent on striving and achievement. She described how aiming for perfection can actually lead to avoidance and procrastination, or to overworking something (such as a piece of art). In extreme cases, with some of the patients she has worked with in a clinical setting, perfectionism has been linked to anxiety, self-harm and eating disorders. Instead, Roz talked about girls broadening and strengthening their sense of self-worth so that it is not just based on achievement, and having a compassionate rather than a self-critical inner-voice – freeing them up to be the best that they can be.

A variety of activities took place during the fortnight, designed to foster a wider perspective in the girls' self-evaluation, and to encourage reflection on perfectionism. The Director of Sixth Form started Day 1 with a very memorable (and amusing!) assembly about attempts to pass her driving test, and what she had learned from her imperfect manoeuvres. Year 7 girls completed an 'achievement log' over the course of a week, in which they focused on one thing every day that was not a typical, measurable achievement (notable examples included 'being happy all day', 'trying Chinese dumplings', 'tidying my room without being asked' and 'phoning grandma'). They also considered helpful and unhelpful patterns of thinking in TLC lessons[1] – something that Year 10 students considered in more detail in an activity about 'all-or-nothing' thinking. The Year 8 students had two CBC (cognitive-behavioural coaching) sessions, in which they reflected on perfectionism, procrastination and setting realistic goals. Year 9 girls completed some of the above activities, and also enjoyed an a Cappella session – seeing the quick progress that could be made and the fun had by having a go at something new. The Year 12 students were joined by Head of Student Counselling at Oxford University, who talked about how the further one goes in academia, they less likely it is that an answer can be verified as being correct or perfect, and hence the importance of developing one's own internal validation. Across the school, different departments also waved goodbye to Little Miss Perfect through varied activities: Sixth Form Chemists discussed the time (wasted) that would be spent aiming to achieve a 100 per cent yield in an experiment, while the Young Enterprise team heard a motivational speaker emphasise the importance of daring to try. In Spanish, younger girls played a game in which they learned that sometimes, although they may 'not yet' have the perfect vocabulary to communicate a message, being prepared to 'have a go' can still be a winning overall result!

The themes of perfectionism and self-esteem are ones that we work on all the time with girls, and will continue to do so. However, we hope that the themed fortnight helped to raise awareness further among girls, parents and staff. In a feedback questionnaire sent to all students, 78 per cent of the girls said that they had thought about the theme of perfectionism or discussed it with friends, staff or family and 64 per cent said that the activities would have an impact on how they would approach things in the future. Of course, not all of the feedback was perfect...so room to learn, hurrah!

Reflections from Dr Sarah Squire in discussion with me (November 2019)

I was privileged to be able to speak with the former Deputy Headteacher of Oxford High School about this project. Sarah's views are her own and represent her personal reflections on the 'Goodbye, Little Miss Perfect' project run while she was working at the school. The following is a summary of the main points from our discussion and are supported by Judith Carlisle, the Headteacher who set up the project.

What prompted the whole-school project?

The context and the values for the project were already in place. As an experienced Head of two high achieving, selective girls' schools, Judith Carlisle was acutely aware of how unhelpful perfectionism could be, both to student wellbeing and to academic progress. As a staff body, earlier in the year, we had been privileged to work with Professors Erica McWilliam and Peter Taylor, who have conducted ground-breaking work on principles to guide teaching and learning. Our work with them led to a shared staff understanding around valuing the importance of welcoming error in the process of rigorous learning, developing classroom cultures which invited uncertainty and designing activities which required students to experience the complex, the unfamiliar and the 'not yet'. This fed into our school's strategic plan, and unhealthy perfectionism certainly wasn't conducive to this approach to learning! We were also aware of the literature around the impact of perfectionism on wellbeing, and it being a 'risk factor' for some mental health conditions. So, the groundwork was already in place, and a serendipitous opportunity arose to launch the project following a conversation with a parent. Judith Carlisle describes a parent saying proudly to her, 'My daughter is such a perfectionist.' Judith had replied by saying, 'Don't worry, we'll soon get that out of her!' The parent was a bit taken aback; Judith recognised that being a perfectionist was widely viewed as being a 'good girl', yet we were aware of potentially negative aspects of perfectionism in young people. Of course, having high standards is a good thing, but striving to achieve unrealistically high standards can cause procrastination and a sense of never feeling satisfied with what one achieves. A short while later, the 'Goodbye, Little Miss Perfect' project was in full swing!

What were the most helpful parts of the project?

The most helpful part was making sure that the whole school community was involved – all departments, all aspects of school life, and students, parents and staff. The project wasn't as an 'add-on' or a novelty, but an integral part of everything we were doing. Staff already had a shared understanding of the principles (outlined earlier) that we were focusing on with our students, and we made use of curriculum lessons, form-time and co-curricular time. We asked department teams to use some of their weekly meeting times to discuss how they would get involved and to feed back their planned activities. Heads of year and tutors planned form times, PSHCE (Personal, Social, Health and Citizenship Education) and assemblies on the theme of perfectionism and based a number of their activities on those described in Roz Shafran's book, *Overcoming Perfectionism*. All of this prompted a lot of creativity and discussions in the staff room!

In terms of 'stand-out' activities, I particularly liked one from an A Level Chemistry class. The students conducted a practical in which they calculated their yield of product and discussed the futility of trying to obtain 100 per cent yield in an experiment because, of course, you can never achieve this, even under 'perfect' lab conditions, never mind in a school lab! They made a poster showing the calculation of their yield, including a drawing of Little Miss Perfect falling off her pedestal in the lab to bring the example to life. At the other end of the age spectrum, and in a language lesson, students were challenged to communicate difficult messages in Spanish as quickly as they could, even though they didn't know all the vocabulary or correct tenses needed. The idea was to push them out of their 'comfort zones' and reward teams for communicating a 'good enough' message, so that they could move on to the next task, rather than trying to get everything perfect.

In form-time the Year 7 students were encouraged to keep an 'achievement log' of things that they were proud of, but which were not related to academic or easily measurable outcomes. They really took to this task, and it was lovely reading their entries with them! Many noted experiences of trying something new, making positive social connections and being responsible around the home. Students began tuning into achievements that were not about striving for something somebody else would necessarily know about; they were things that prompted internal pride and satisfaction. I think, for this reason, this was probably my favourite activity.

In terms of co-curricular events, a highlight was an open a Cappella session, for anyone who wanted to have a go. It was led by a teacher who ran an elite a Capella group whose talent was much admired among the students. The open session filled the room! Girls came to have a go because they thought it looked fun, not because they were brilliant singers, or because they were committing to it for a term, or striving to take part in a concert, or pass a singing exam!

What were the less helpful parts of the project?

Inevitably, some activities may have been more helpful than others. However, I think everything we did was valuable because that part of the message to our students needed to be that staff were taking 'risks' too – we had planned things carefully and had coordinated what we believed would be fun and helpful activities (after all, we had very high standards!) but we needed to role model welcoming error and uncertainty in our own learning too. I believe that the collaborative conversations which followed between staff and students in terms of 'what worked well' and what would be 'even better if' were a valuable component of the project.

It is quite difficult to evaluate what was most helpful. It's easy to identify the most memorable activities – perhaps those which generated most conversation, or photos and posters which were then displayed – but I believe (and have evidence from subsequent lesson observations) that some of the more subtle and ongoing activities within classrooms had considerable impact. And, of course, each student is different, so what worked for one might not have worked for another. It's important to emphasise that, while perfectionism held a particularly high profile in the school community during the time of focused activities, the work tackling unhelpful perfectionism was ongoing both before and after this.

How easy was it to get staff 'on board' with the project?

With any initiative there will be some challenges – teachers are very busy people and, understandably, sometimes feel concerned that an initiative might require a lot of additional planning time. My experience is that they also have high standards themselves, so want their activities to be really effective! However, staff were already very aware of the manifestations of perfectionism among students (the student who can't get started on an essay, the one who keeps correcting the first sentence, the one who spends far too long on an open-ended homework, or on posting the perfect Instagram). There was 'buy-in' from staff because of the work we had already done with Professors Erica McWilliam and Peter Taylor, identifying the importance of welcoming error in learning. When we decided to have a particular focus on the theme of perfectionism, this context provided genuine motivation among staff. As the project gained momentum, I felt there was also a real sense of pride among colleagues in how they were interpreting the theme in their lessons and activities; there was a lot of idea-sharing in the staff room. Roz Shafran had even asked for some examples of the activities we had been doing for her keynote lecture, which provided a healthy sense of competition!

How easy was it to get parents 'on board' with the project?

We were fortunate to have a very supportive and intelligent parent body. They were very interested in the project, and also had questions about it. Roz Shafran kindly agreed to give a lecture to the school community, lending academic gravitas to what we were doing and providing an expert's overview of the research on perfectionism. Of course, not all parents were able to attend the lecture, and meanwhile the media interest was phenomenal! It became very high-profile, very quickly, in a way we hadn't anticipated (Judith Carlisle was invited to speak on the *Today* programme on Radio 4 almost immediately!) and this posed some challenges. Inevitably, aspects of our project were reported slightly inaccurately in the written press, and we needed to do a bit of repair work with some parents who appeared a little concerned that we might be lowering standards, or pre-empting less excellent exam results! There were, of course, also advantages to the media coverage; it felt as if there was a national conversation around perfectionism and, since then, Judith has also been invited to speak internationally about the topic. As school leaders, we also didn't necessarily want to have 'cosy' projects, but something that initiated interest, discussion and debate. Back to where we started in agreeing the principles we wanted to establish for our students!

What is the lasting impact of this work?

I think it's fair to say that the full impact of any intervention at school may not be evident within a student's school years. The long-term impact will be far more important than any short-term impact, yet difficult to ascertain. When I've had conversations with parents around this, they have identified with the suggestion that we would really need to ask students in ten or 20 years' time! Having said that, it is important to try to assess impact, and I have some formal feedback from students about impact (via a questionnaire sent to all students) and more anecdotal feedback.

From the questionnaire, around two-thirds of students reported that the project had had an impact on how they would approach things in the future and over three-quarters reported that they had talked about perfectionism and our school project with friends and family. I was particularly pleased with the latter finding, because we all know that talking about something with others and being questioned about it in your wider social setting really makes you think about it and maintains the ongoing dialogue around the topic.

My more anecdotal evidence for impact comes from a variety of sources. For example, when observing an A-Level Economics class, I witnessed a student volunteer to go through a (partial) answer on the board in front of the class. Although she had not managed to complete the problem she stood up in front of the class, saying 'I haven't managed to work out the last bit of this question, but can I go through where I've got to and then maybe everyone can help with the last part?' The language of not being there 'yet' seemed to become much more embedded in our school as a result of the project. My second anecdotal evidence of impact is very different – it comes from the school panto! Every year, the tradition was that the students wrote the script of a pantomime, which the staff performed. We know that if something makes it into the pantomime – even if it is the butt of some jokes – then the message is embedded. I am pleased to report that Little Miss Perfect made several appearances and references to her unhelpful tendencies still continue to appear in the script!

Any advice to other schools wanting to try this approach?

I would advise being very clear why you are doing a project like this and what you mean by perfectionism (e.g. are you looking at unrealistically high standards the person places on themselves, or on others?). Is perfectionism genuinely an issue among your student population, and is there motivation among the school community to address it? If someone is achieving high standards without it having a shadow on their wellbeing or performance (or that of others) then there might not be an issue! So, I think you have to be really clear about what you are trying to tackle and why, and the outcome you are hoping for. A short project won't work in isolation, so think about how the whole-school community is engaged in order to achieve maximum impact. An effective project needs to be holistic and integral to the way of life in school; it is so powerful when staff, students and parents share a common language and 'short-hand' for some of the key messages ('Is it good enough to allow you to move on to the next thing?' or 'That sounds a bit "all-or-nothing" to me!'). Don't forget that students can be a fantastic support to other students, so think about how they will engage in activities and conversations with each other, not just with the adults around them.

There is accessible literature on perfectionism, based on good research, that can be usefully shared with interested students, staff and parents and being familiar with this will enable school leaders to answer questions based on evidence. I feel it's really important to translate good research from academic psychology into 'real-life' communities, such as schools, without it becoming too oversimplified, so have some of the literature to hand to share.

And finally, don't worry if your project is not perfect! I should end by sharing that on the final day of our 'Goodbye Little Miss Perfect' activities, we had an outbreak of norovirus at school. So many students and staff became unwell that we had to close the school. So that wasn't a perfect ending!

Endnotes

1   TLC was a course which helped girls in Key Stage 3 develop and explore different skills and approaches to their thinking and learning, and provided opportunities for them to be more creative regarding technology and computing. TLC represented Thinking/Technology, Learning/Linking, Computing/Communication.

Appendix E: Assess-Plan-Do-Review Cycle

ASSESS

Consider who you may need to be concerned about.

Look out for possible signs and symptoms.

What is and is not working well for this young person?

What are their main strengths and difficulties?

What might be the underlying need?

How aware are they of the 'problem'? Are they motivated to change?

PLAN

Where do you want the young person to get to – what skills or behaviours do you want to see?

What approach could you use to help them get there? How will you do this? When? How often? How will you know if it is working? Who else can help?

DO

Try out the strategies!

REVIEW

What progress is being made towards the target?

Are things getting better, worse or staying the same?

Are any changes needed? How will these be made?

Are there any other young people we can also support based on what we have learned from this cycle?

Appendix F: 'What to Do If You Are Concerned': A Flowchart for Schools

Young person acknowledges problem

- Agree with the young person the target for change and identify possible barriers (e.g. see Chapter 3)
- Agree with the young person who is the best person to help and what could be helpful

Young person does not acknowledge problem

- Monitor in school
- Liaise with parents

School-based support

- 1:1
- Groupwork
- Meeting with family

External support

- Child and Adolescent Mental Health Services
- School/Educational Psychologist
- Family Doctor, School Nurse

Systemic support

- Whole-school approach to teaching and learning: growth mindset and resiliency
- Anti-perfectionism campaign (e.g. 'Goodbye Mr/Little Miss Perfect')

In all situations

- Record-keeping: concerns, conversations, actions
- Respect confidentiality: policy and safeguarding procedures
- Debrief with colleague, manager or external professional

References

Achtziger, A. and Bayer, U.C. (2013) 'Self-control mediates the link between perfectionism and stress.' *Motivation and Emotion 37*, 3, 413–423.

Adams, L.A. and Govender, K. (2008) '"Making a Perfect Man": Traditional masculine ideology and perfectionism among adolescent boys.' *South African Journal of Psychology 38*, 3, 551–562.

Adelson, J.L. and Wilson, H.E. (2009) *Letting Go of Perfect: Overcoming Perfectionism in Kids*. Waco, TX: Prufrock Press Inc.

Affrunti, N. and Woodruff-Borden, J. (2014) 'Perfectionism in pediatric anxiety and depressive disorders.' *Clinical Child and Family Psychology Review 17*, 3, 299–317.

Afshar, H., Roohafza, H., Sadeghi, M., Saadaty, A. *et al.* (2011) 'Positive and negative perfectionism and their relationship with anxiety and depression in Iranian school students.' *Journal of Research in Medical Sciences: The Official Journal of Isfahan University of Medical Sciences 16*, 1, 79–86.

Albano, A.M., Chorpita, B.F. and Barlow, D.H. (2003) 'Childhood anxiety disorders.' *Child Psychopathology 2*, 279–329.

American Academy of Pediatrics (2014) 'High-achievers and perfectionists.' Accessed on 28 November 2015 at www.healthychildren.org/English/ages-stages/young-adult/Pages/High-Achievers-and-Perfectionists.aspx.

Arpin-Cribbie, C.A., Irvine, J., Ritvo, P., Cribbie, R.A., Flett, G.L. and Hewitt, P.L. (2008) 'Perfectionism and psychological distress: A modeling approach to understanding their therapeutic relationship.' *Journal of Rational-Emotive and Cognitive-Behavioral Therapy 26*, 3, 151–167.

Arrazzini Stewart, M. and De George-Walker, L. (2014) 'Self-handicapping, perfectionism, locus of control and self-efficacy: A path model.' *Personality and Individual Differences 66*, 160–164.

Ashby, J.S., Kottman, T. and Martin, J.L. (2004) 'Play therapy with young perfectionists.' *International Journal of Play Therapy 13*, 1, 35–55.

Atkinson, L., Quarrington, B., Cyr, J.J. and Atkinson, F.V. (1989) 'Differential classification in school refusal.' *British Journal of Psychiatry 155*, 191–195.

Azevedo, M.H., Bos, S.C., Soares, M.J., Marques, M., Pereira, A.T., Maia, B. and Macedo, A. (2010) 'Longitudinal study on perfectionism and sleep disturbance.' *World Journal of Biological Psychiatry 11*, 2, 476–485.

BBC News (2015) 'Child mental health: Parents to get more say on care, says NHS.' Accessed on 20 February 2015 at www.bbc.co.uk/news/health-31529674.

Beevers, C.G. and Miller, I.W. (2004) 'Perfectionism, cognitive bias, and hopelessness as prospective predictors of suicidal ideation.' *Suicide and Life-Threatening Behavior 34*, 2, 126–137.

Bell, J., Stanley, N., Mallon, S. and Manthorpe, J. (2010) 'The role of perfectionism in student suicide: Three case studies from the UK.' *OMEGA: The Journal of Death and Dying 61*, 3, 251–267.

Bennathan, M., Boxall, M. and Colley, D. (1998) *The Boxall Profile for Young People: Assessment and Intervention at Secondary Stage*. London: The Nurture Group Network.

Ben-Shahar, T. (2009) *The Pursuit of Perfect*. Berkshire: McGraw-Hill.

Ben-Shahar, T. (2008) *Happier*. Berkshire: McGraw-Hill.

Besharat, M.A., Azizi, K. and Poursharifi, H. (2011) 'The relationship between parenting styles and children's perfectionism in a sample of Iranian families.' *Procedia Social and Behavioural Sciences 15*, 1276–1279.

Blankstein, K. and Lumley, C. (2015) 'Multidimensional perfectionism and ruminative brooding in current dysphoria, anxiety, worry and anger.' *Journal of Rational-Emotive and Cognitive-Behavior Therapy 26*, 1–26.

Bolton, J.M., Cox, B.J., Afifi, T.O., Enns, M.W., Bienvenu, O.J. and Sareen, J. (2008) 'Anxiety disorders and risk for suicide attempts: Findings from the Baltimore Epidemiologic Catchment Area follow-up study.' *Depression and Anxiety 25*, 477–489.

Boone, L., Claes, L. and Luyten, P. (2014) 'Too strict or too loose? Perfectionism and impulsivity: The relation with eating disorder symptoms using a person-centered approach.' *Eating Behaviors 15*, 1, 17–23.

Boone, L., Soenens, B., Mouratidis, A., Vansteenkiste, M, Verstuyf, J. and Braet, C. (2012) 'Daily fluctuations in perfectionism dimensions and their relation to eating disorder symptoms.' *Journal of Research in Personality 46*, 6, 678–687.

Booth, R. (2016) 'Tackling mental illness early: The people being taught to spot warning signs.' Accessed on 15 February 2016 at www.theguardian.com/society/2016/jan/25/warning-signs-early-intervention-mental-illness-symptoms-health.

Bould, H. (2016) 'Eating disorders are more common in some schools than others – but why?' Accessed on 29 April 2016 at www.theguardian.com/science/sifting-the-evidence/2016/apr/28/eating-disorders-are-more-common-in-some-schools-than-others-but-why?CMP=Share_iOSApp_Other.

British Psychological Society (2016) 'Psychological therapies staff in the NHS report alarming levels of depression and stress – their own.' [Press release.]

Buchanan, M. (2015) 'Children's mental health services "cut by £50m".' Accessed on 20 February 2015 at www.bbc.co.uk/news/education-30735370.

Buhlmann, U., Etcoff, N.L. and Wilhelm, S. (2008) Facial attractiveness ratings and perfectionism in body dysmorphic disorder and obsessive-compulsive disorder. *Journal of Anxiety Disorders, 22*(3), 540–547.

Burgess, K. (2015) 'Tragedy of the A-grade schoolboy.' Accessed on 20 February 2015 at www.thetimes.co.uk/tto/news/uk/article4358662.ece.

Burnam, A., Komarraju, M., Hamel, R. and Nadler, D.R. (2014) 'Do adaptive perfectionism and self-determined motivation reduce academic procrastination?' *Learning and Individual Differences 36*, 165–172.

Burns, E.F. (2008) *Nobody's Perfect: A Story for Children about Perfectionism.* APA: Magination.

Burns, J. (2015a) 'Children's mental health is parents' greatest concern.' Accessed on 20 February 2015 at www.bbc.co.uk/news/education-30701591.

Burns, J. (2015b) 'More pupils have mental health issues, say school staff.' Accessed on 12 December 2015 at www.bbc.co.uk/news/education-32075251.

Carter, T., Walker, G., Aubeeluck, A. and Manning, J. (2018) 'Assessment tools of immediate risk of self-harm and suicide in children and young people: A scoping review.' *Journal of Child Health Care 23*, 2, 178–199.

Casale, S., Fioravanti, G., Flett, G.L. and Hewitt, P.L. (2014) 'From socially prescribed perfectionism to problematic use of internet communicative services: The mediating roles of perceived social support and the fear of negative evaluation.' *Addictive Behaviors 39*, 12, 1816–1822.

Cattell, H. and Mead, A. (2008) 'The sixteen personality factor questionnaire (16PF).' *The SAGE Handbook of Personality Theory and Assessment 2*, 135–159.

Chan, D.W. (2012) 'Life satisfaction among highly achieving students in Hong Kong: Do gratitude and the "good-enough mindset" add to the contribution of perfectionism in prediction?' *Educational Psychology 32*, 5, 613–626.

Chan, D.W. (2009) 'Dimensionality and typology of perfectionism: The use of the Frost Multidimensional Perfectionism Scale with Chinese gifted students in Hong Kong.' *Gifted Child Quarterly 53*, 3, 174–187.

Chan, D.W. (2007) 'Perfectionism among Chinese gifted students in Hong Kong: Relationships to coping strategies and teacher ratings.' *Gifted Education International 23*, 3, 289–300.

Cheney, G., Schlosser, A., Nash, P. and Glover, L. (2014) 'Targeted group-based interventions in schools to promote emotional well-being: A systematic review.' *Clinical Child Psychology and Psychiatry 19*, 3, 412–438.

Cohn, P. (2013) 'Is Serena Williams a perfectionsist.' Sports Psychology for Tennis. Accessed on 10 January 2020 at www.sportspsychologytennis.com/is-serena-williams-a-perfectionist.

Collingwood, J. (2018) 'The Importance of Personal Boundaries.' Accessed on 1 April 2020 at https://psychcentral.com/lib/the-importance-of-personal-boundaries.

Comerchero, V. (2008) 'Gender, tenure status, teacher efficacy, perfectionism and teacher burnout.' Accessed on 12 December 2019 at https://pqdtopen.proquest.com/doc/304651968.html?FMT=ABS.

Conners, C., Sitarenios, G., Parker, J. and Epstein, J. (1998) 'The Revised Conners' Parent Rating Scale (CPRS-R): Factor structure, reliability, and criterion validity.' Journal of Abnormal Child Psychology 26, 4, 257–268.

Cooke, J. (2014) 'Mental health services cuts "affecting children".' Accessed on 20 February 2015 at www.bbc.co.uk/news/health-27942416.

Coren, S.A. and Luthar, S.S. (2014) 'Pursuing perfection: Distress and interpersonal functioning among adolescent boys in single-sex and co-educational independent schools.' Psychology in the Schools 51, 9, 931–946.

Corry, J., Green, M.J., Roberts, G., Frankland, A. et al. (2013) 'Anxiety, stress and perfectionism in bipolar disorder.' Journal of Affective Disorders 151, 1016–1024.

Coughlin, J.W. and Kalodner, C. (2006) 'Media literacy as a prevention intervention for college women at low- or high-risk for eating disorders.' Body Image: An International Journal of Research 3, 35–43.

Crowne, D.P. and Marlowe, D. (1960) 'A new scale of social desirability independent of psychopathology.' Journal of Consulting Psychology 24, 349–354.

Dahl, M. (2014) 'The alarming new research on perfectionism.' Accessed on 4 March 2015 at www.nymag.com/scienceofus/2014/09/alarming-new-research-on-perfectionism.html.

Daigneault, S.D. (1999) 'Narrative means to Adlerian ends: An illustrated comparison of narrative therapy and Adlerian play therapy.' Journal of Individual Psychology 55, 298–315.

Damian, L.E., Stoeber, J., Negru, O. and Baban, A. (2014) 'Perfectionism and achievement goal orientations in adolescent school students.' Psychology in the Schools 51, 9, 960–971.

Davies, W. (2013) 'Davies's structured interview for assessing adolescents in crisis.' Accessed on 3 November 2019 at www.nice.org.uk/sharedlearning/davies-s-structured-interview-for-assessing-adolescents-in-crisis.

Deci, E. and Ryan, R. (2002) Handbook of Self-Determination Research. Rochester, NY: University of Rochester Press.

DeSocio, J. and Hootman, J. (2004) 'Children's mental health and school success.' Journal of School Nursing 20, 4, 189–196.

DfE (2014) SEND Code of Practice: 0–25 years. Accessed on 11 March 2015 at www.gov.uk/government/publications/send-code-of-practice-0-to-25.

DiBartolo, P.M., Frost, R.O., Chang, P., LaSota, M. and Grills, A.E. (2004) 'Shedding light on the relationship between personal standards and psychopathology: The case for conditional self-worth.' *Journal of Rational-Emotive and Cognitive-Behaviour Therapy, 22,* 241–254.

DiBartolo, P.M., Yen, L.C. and Frost, R. (2008) 'How do the dimensions of perfectionism relate to mental health?' *Cognitive Therapy and Research 32,* 401–417.

DiPrima, A.J., Ashby, J.S., Gnilka, P.B. and Noble, C.L. (2011) 'Family relationships and perfectionism in middle-school students.' *Psychology in the Schools 48,* 8, 815–827.

Donaldson, D., Spirito, A. and Farnett, E. (2000) 'The role of perfectionism and depressive cognitions in understanding the hopelessness experienced by adolescent suicide attempters.' *Child Psychiatry and Human Development 31,* 99–111.

Dour, H.J. and Theran, S.A. (2011) 'The interaction between the superhero ideal and maladaptive perfectionism as predictors of unhealthy eating attitudes and body esteem.' *Body Image 8,* 93–96.

Dweck, C.S. (2006) *Mindset: The New Psychology of Success.* New York: Random House.

Egan, S.J., van Noort, E., Chee, A., Kane, R.T., Hoiles, K.J., Shafran, R. and Wade, T.D. (2014) 'A randomised controlled trial of face to face versus pure online self-help cognitive behavioural treatment for perfectionism.' *Behaviour Research and Therapy 63,* 107–113.

Egan, S.J., Wade, T.D. and Shafran, R. (2011) 'Perfectionism as a transdiagnostic process: A clinical review.' *Clinical Psychology Review 31,* 203–212.

Emotion Coaching UK (2019) 'What is Emotional Coaching?' Accessed on 1 April 2020 at https://www.emotioncoachinguk.com/what-is-emotion-coaching.

Enns, M.W., Cox, B.J. and Clara, I. (2002) 'Adaptive and maladaptive perfectionism: Developmental origins and association with depression proneness.' *Personality and Individual Differences 33,* 921–935.

Essau, C.A., Leung, P.W., Conradt, J., Cheng, H. and Wong, T. (2008) 'Anxiety symptoms in Chinese and German adolescents: Their relationship with early learning experiences, perfectionism, and learning motivation.' *Depression and Anxiety 25,* 801–810.

Fletcher, K., Yang, Y., Johnson, S.L., Berk, M. *et al.* (2019) 'Buffering against maladaptive perfectionism in bipolar disorder: The role of self-compassion.' *Journal of Affective Disorders 250,* 132–139.

Flett, G. (2014) 'Perfectionism as a risk factor in suicide.' Accessed on 5 February 2015 at www.bps.org.uk/news/perfectionism-risk-factor-suicide.

Flett, G.L., Coulter, L.-M. and Hewitt, P.L. (2012) 'The Perfectionistic Self-Presentation Scale-Junior Form psychometric properties and association with social anxiety in early adolescents.' *Canadian Journal of School Psychology* 27, 2, 136–149.

Flett, G.L., Druckman, T., Hewitt, P.L. and Wekerle, C. (2012) 'Perfectionism, coping, social support, and depression in maltreated adolescents.' *Journal of Rational-Emotive and Cognitive-Behaviour Therapy* 30, 2, 118–131.

Flett, G.L. and Hewitt, P.L. (2014) 'A proposed framework for preventing perfectionism and promoting resilience and mental health among vulnerable children and adolescent.' *Psychology in the Schools* 51, 9, 899–912.

Flett, G.L. and Hewitt, P.L. (2012) 'Perfectionism and cognitive factors in distress and dysfunction in children and adolescents: Introduction to the special issue.' *Journal of Rational-Emotive and Cognitive-Behavior Therapy* 30, 2, 53–61.

Flett, G.L. and Hewitt, P.L. (2008) 'Treatment interventions for perfectionism – a cognitive perspective: Introduction to the Special Issue.' *Journal of Rational-Emotive and Cognitive-Behavior Therapy* 26, 3, 127–133.

Flett, G.L., Hewitt, P.L., Besser, A., Su, C. *et al.* (2016) 'The Child–Adolescent Perfectionism Scale: Development, psychometric properties, and associations with stress, distress, and psychiatric symptoms.' *Journal of Psychoeducational Assessment* 34, 7, 634–652.

Flett, G.L., Hewitt, P.L. and Cheng, W.M.W. (2008) 'Perfectionism, distress, and irrational beliefs in high school students: Analyses with an abbreviated Survey of Personal Beliefs for adolescents.' *Journal of Rational-Emotive and Cognitive-Behavior Therapy* 26, 3, 194–205.

Folksy, T. (2014) 'Heartbreaking: Teen worried about exam results left chilling note for parents before committing suicide.' Accessed on 20 February 2015 at www.passnownow.com/heartbroken-teen-worried-about-exam-results-left-chilling-note-for-parents-before-committing-suicide.

Franko, D.L., Striegel-Moore, R.H., Barton, B.A., Schumann, B.C., Garner, D.M., Daniels, S.R. and Crawford, P.B. (2004) 'Measuring eating concerns in Black and White adolescent girls.' *International Journal of Eating Disorders* 35, 2, 179–189.

Freud, A. (1937) *The Ego and the Mechanisms of Defence.* London: Hogarth Press and Institute of Psycho-Analysis.

Friedman, R.A. (2006) 'Uncovering an epidemic – screening for mental illness in teens.' *New England Journal of Medicine* 355, 2717–2719.

Frontier Performance (2019) 'Cristiano Ronaldo's lesson on perfectionism (and how you can use it to excel at sales).' Accessed on 3 November 2019 at www.frontierp.com/au/cristiano-ronaldos-lesson-perfectionism-can-use-excel-sales.

Frost, R.O., Marten, P., Lahart, C. and Rosenblate, R. (1990) 'The dimensions of perfectionism.' *Cognitive Therapy and Research 14*, 449–468.

Fung, C.H.M. (2009) 'Asperger's and musical creativity: The case of Erik Satie.' *Personality and Individual Differences 46*, 8, 775–783.

Fusun, Y. and Cemrenur, T. (2014) 'The study of teacher candidates' perfectionism in relation with achievement and demographics.' *Procedia – Social and Behavioral Sciences 152*, 121–126.

Gaultiere, B. (2000/2012) 'Self-Assessment Perfectionism Screening Test.' Accessed on 5 November 2019 at https://medicine.llu.edu/sites/medicine.llu.edu/files/docs/self-assessment-perfectionism-test.pdf.

Gilbert, P. (2002) 'Understanding the biopsychosocial approach II: Individual and social interventions.' *Clinical Psychology 15*, 28–32.

Gilman, R., Adams, R. and Nounopoulos, A. (2011) 'The interpersonal relationships and social perceptions of adolescent perfectionists.' *Journal of Research on Adolescence 21*, 2, 505–511.

Gnilka, P.B., Ashby, J. and Noble, C.M. (2012) 'Multidimensional perfectionism and anxiety: Differences among individuals with perfectionism and tests of a coping-mediation model.' *Journal of Counseling and Development 90*, 4, 437–436.

Greenaway, R. and Howlin, P. (2010) 'Dysfunctional attitudes and perfectionism and their relationship to anxious and depressive symptoms in boys with Autism Spectrum Disorders.' *Journal of Autism and Developmental Disorders 40*, 10, 1179–1187.

Greenspon, T.S. (2014) 'Is there an antidote to perfectionism?' *Psychology in the Schools 51*, 9, 986–998.

Greenspon, T.S. (2000) '"Healthy perfectionism" is an oxymoron! Reflections on the psychology of perfectionism and the sociology of science.' *The Journal of Secondary Gifted Education 11*, 4, 197–208, 222–223.

Greig, A. and MacKay, T. (2013) *The Homunculi Approach to Social and Emotional Wellbeing: A Flexible CBT Programme for Young People on the Autism Spectrum or with Emotional and Behavioural Difficulties.* London: Jessica Kingsley Publishers.

Guardian, The (2015) 'Trump under fire: Will "perfectionist" fold at debate without polling lead?' Accessed on 5 November 2019 at www.theguardian.com/us-news/2015/oct/28/donald-trump-republican-debate-polling.

Guardian, The (2014) 'Secret teacher: We're part of the reason students are suffering from more stress.' Accessed on 4 December 2015 at www.theguardian.com/teacher-network/teacher-blog/2014/feb/22/secret-teacher-student-stress-suffering.

Guerra, N.G. and Bradshaw, C.P. (2008) 'Linking the prevention of problem behaviours and positive youth development: Core competencies for positive youth development and risk prevention.' *New Directions for Child and Adolescent Development 122*, 1–17.

Hamachek, D.E. (1978) 'Psychodynamics of normal and neurotic perfectionism.' *Psychology 15*, 27–33.

Haring, M., Hewitt, P.L. and Flett, G.L. (2003) 'Perfectionism, coping, and quality of intimate relationships.' *Journal of Marriage and Family 65*, 1, 143–158.

Harper, D. (2016) 'Beyond individual therapy.' Accessed on 5 November 2019 at www.thepsychologist.bps.org.uk/volume-29/june/beyond-individual-therapy.

Hartley-Brewer, E. (2015) 'Pressure is making young people insecure.' Accessed on 20 February 2015 at www.thetimes.co.uk/tto/health/news/article4358665.ece.

Hasse, A.M., Prapavessis, H. and Owens, R.G. (2002) 'Perfectionism, social physique anxiety and disordered eating: A comparison of male and female elite athletes.' *Psychology of Sport and Exercise 3*, 3, 209–222.

Hewitt, P.L., Blasberg, J.S., Flett, G.L., Besser, A., Sherry, S.B., Caelian, C. and Birch, S. (2011) 'Perfectionistic self-presentation in children and adolescents: Development and validation of the Perfectionistic Self-Presentation Scale – Junior Form.' *Psychological Assessment 23*, 1, 125–142.

Hewitt, P.L., Caelian, C.F., Flett, G.L., Sherry, S.B., Collins, L. and Flynn, C.A. (2002) 'Perfectionism in children: Associations with depression, anxiety, and anger.' *Personality and Individual Differences 32*, 1049–1061.

Hewitt, P.L. and Flett, G.L. (2004) *Multidimensional Perfectionism Scale (MPS): Technical Manual.* Toronto, Canada: Mutli-Health Systems.

Hewitt, P.L. and Flett, G.L. (1991) 'Perfectionism in the self and social contexts: Conceptualization, assessment and association with psychopathology.' *Journal of Personality and Social Psychology 60*, 3, 456–470.

Hollender, M.H. (1978) 'Perfectionism: A neglected personality trait.' *Journal of Clinical Psychology 39*, 384.

Hopkins, E. (2018) 'D12's Kuniva explains how perfectionist Eminem would take people off songs.' Accessed on 5 November 2019 at www.edmhoney.com/d12s-kuniva-explains-how-perfectionist-eminem-would-take-people-off-songs.

Independent, The (2009) 'Eminem: The fall and rise of a superstar.' Accessed on 5 November 2019 at www.independent.co.uk/arts-entertainment/music/features/eminem-the-fall-and-rise-of-a-superstar-1544787.html.

Jackson, M. (2004) 'Exam stress can lead to suicide.' Accessed on 20 February 2015 at www.news.bbc.co.uk/1/hi/health/3758359.stm

Jaradat, A.-K.M. (2013) 'Multidimensional perfectionism in a sample of Jordanian high school students.' *Australian Journal of Guidance and Counselling 23*, 1, 95–105.

Jowett, G.E., Hill, A.P., Hall, H.K. and Curran, T. (2016) 'Perfectionism, burnout and engagement in youth sport: The mediating role of basic psychological needs.' *Psychology of Sport and Exercise 24*, 18–26.

Kearns, H., Forbes, A. and Gardiner, M. (2007) 'A cognitive behavioural coaching intervention for the treatment of perfectionism and self-handicapping in a non-clinical population.' *Behaviour Change 24*, 3, 157–172.

Klibert, J., Lamis, D.A., Collins, W., Smalley, K.B., Warren, J.C., Yancey, C.T. and Winterowd, C. (2014) 'Resilience mediates the relations between perfectionism and college student distress.' *Journal of Counseling and Development 92*, 1, 75–82.

Koval, J. (1978) *A Complete Guide to Therapy.* London: Penguin Group.

Kowal, A. and Pritchard, D. (1990) 'Psychological characteristics of children who suffer from headache: A research note.' *Journal of Child Psychology and Psychiatry 31*, 637–649.

Kunin, J. (2017) 'Focus on achievement is destroying education: Opinion.' Accessed on 5 November 2019 at www.thestar.com/opinion/commentary/2017/06/26/focus-on-achievement-is-destroying-education-opinion.html.

Kutcher, S. and Chehil, S. (2007) 'Tool for Assessment of Suicide Risk (TASR).' Accessed on 5 November 2019 at www.onlinelibrary.wiley.com/doi/pdf/10.1002/9780470750933.app2.

Kutlesa, N. and Arthur N. (2008) 'Overcoming negative aspects of perfectionism through group treatment.' *Journal of Rational-Emotive and Cognitive-Behavior Therapy 26*, 3, 134–150.

Låftman, S.B., Almquist, Y.B. and Östberg, V. (2013) 'Students' accounts of school-performance stress: A qualitative analysis of a high-achieving setting in Stockholm, Sweden.' *Journal of Youth Studies 16*, 7, 932–949.

Lee, M., Roberts-Collins, C., Coughtrey, A., Philips, L. and Shafran, R. (2011) 'Behavioural expressions, imagery and perfectionism.' *Behavioural and Cognitive Psychotherapy 39*, 4, 413–425.

Leung, F., Wang, J. and Tang, C.W. (2004) 'Psychometric properties and normative data of the Eating Disorder Inventory among 12 to 18 year old Chinese girls in Hong Kong.' *Journal of Psychosomatic Research 57*, 1, 59–66.

Lindberg, F.H. and Distad, L.J. (1985) 'Survival responses to incest: Adolescents in crisis.' *Child Abuse and Neglect 9*, 521–526.

Lippman, B.L. (2012) 'Problematizing perfectionism: A closer look at the perfectionism construct.' Accessed on 19 February 2016 at https://wp.nyu.edu/steinhardt-appsych_opus/problematizing-perfectionism-a-closer-look-at-the-perfectionism-construct.

Lloyd, S., Schmidt, U., Khondoker, M. and Tchanturia, K. (2015) 'Can psychological interventions reduce perfectionism? A systematic review and meta-analysis.' *Behavioural and Cognitive Psychotherapy 43*, 6, 705–731.

Longbottom, J. (2016) 'Suicide rates for young Australians highest in 10 years, researchers call for new prevention strategies.' Accessed on 5 November 2019 at www.abc.net.au/news/2016-11-30/system-for-suicide-prevention-rates-highest-10-years/8076780.

Lundh, L. (2004) 'Perfectionism and acceptance.' *Journal of Rational-Emotive and Cognitive-Behavior Therapy 22*, 4, 255–269.

Lyman, E.L. and Luthar, S.S. (2014) 'Further evidence on the "costs of privilege": Perfectionism in high-achieving youth at socioeconomic extremes.' *Psychology in the Schools 51*, 9, 913–930.

Mackinnon, S.P., Sherry, S.B. and Pratt, M.W. (2013) 'The relationship between perfectionism, agency, and communion: A longitudinal mixed methods analysis.' *Journal of Research in Personality 47*, 263–271.

Mahnken, K. (2017) 'The hidden mental health crisis in America's schools: Millions of kids not receiving services they need.' Accessed on 5 November 2019 at www.the74million.org/the-hidden-mental-health-crisis-in-americas-schools-millions-of-kids-not-receiving-services-they-need.

Mallinson, S.H., Hill, A.P., Hall, H.K. and Gotwals, J.K. (2014) 'The 2x2 model of perfectionism and school- and community-based sport participation.' *Psychology in the Schools 51*, 9, 972–985.

Manning, M. (2017) 'Mental health in schools.' Accessed on 5 November 2019 at www.amhp.org.au/2017/mental-health-in-schools.

March, J.S., Parker, J.D., Sullivan, K., Stallings, P. and Conners, C.K. (1997) 'The Multidimensional Anxiety Scale for Children (MASC): Factor structure, reliability, and validity.' *Journal of the American Academy of Child and Adolescent Psychiatry 36*, 597–614.

Maslow, A. (1970) *Motivation and Personality* (2nd ed.). New York: Harper and Row.

McConnell, G. (2016) 'The highest rate of teen suicide in the developed world.' Accessed on 5 November 2019 at www.stuff.co.nz/national/health/85305366/the-highest-rate-of-teen-suicide-in-the-developed-world.

McVey, G.L., Davis, R., Tweed, S. and Shaw, B.F. (2004) 'Evaluation of a school-based program designed to improve body image satisfaction, global self-esteem, and eating attitudes and behaviors: A replication study.' *International Journal of Eating Disorders 36*, 1, 1–11.

McWhinnie, C.M., Abela, J.R., Knauper, B. and Zhang, C. (2009) 'Development and validation of the revised Children's Dysfunctional Attitudes Scale.' *British Journal of Clinical Psychology 48*, 3, 287–308.

Meradji, P. (2018) 'Bringing mental health to the forefront of education.' Accessed on 16 October 2019 at www.psychcentral.com/blog/bringing-mental-health-to-the-forefront-of-education.

Miron, O., Yu, K.H., Wilf-Miron, R. and Kohane, I.S. (2019) 'Suicide rates among adolescents and young adults in the United States, 2000–2017.' Accessed on 5 November 2019 at www.jamanetwork.com/journals/jama/article-abstract/2735809.

Mofield, E.L. and Chakraborti-Ghosh, S. (2010) 'Addressing multidimensional perfectionism in gifted adolescents with affective curriculum.' *Journal for the Education of the Gifted 33*, 4, 479–513.

Mohdin, A. (2018) 'Suicide rate rises among young people in England and Wales.' Accessed on 5 November 2019 at www.theguardian.com/society/2018/sep/04/suicide-rate-rises-among-young-people-in-england-and-wales.

Moon, T.R. (2006) 'Teaching to the test and gifted learners.' Accessed on 1 April 2020 at https://blogs.tip.duke.edu/giftedtoday/2006/05/29/teaching-to-the-test-and-gifted-learners.

Morris, L. and Lomax, C. (2014) 'Review: Assessment, development and treatment of childhood perfectionism: a systematic review.' *Child and Adolescent Mental Health 19*, 4, 225–234.

Natcharian, L. (2010) 'Real learning: Meet the perfectionists.' Accessed on 30 November 2015 at www.blog.masslive.com/real_learning/2010/07/meet_the_perfectionists.html.

Nauert, R. (2014) 'Perfectionism linked to suicide.' Accessed on 5 February 2015 at www.psychcentral.com/news/2014/09/26/perfectionism-linked-to-suicide/75399.html.

Neumeister, K.L.S. (2004) 'Understanding the relationship between perfectionism and achievement motivation in gifted college students.' *Gifted Child Quarterly 48*, 219–231.

Neumeister, K.L.S. (2003) 'Perfectionism in gifted college students: Family influences and implications for achievement.' *Roeper Review 26*, 1, 53.

Neumeister, K.L.S. and Finch, H. (2006) 'Perfectionism in high-ability students: Relational precursors and influences on achievement motivation.' *Gifted Child Quarterly 50*, 3, 238–251.

Nolan, J. (2014) 'Perfectionism is a mental illness and it's ruining my life.' Accessed on 25 November 2015 at www.vice.com/en_uk/read/how-perfectionism-destroyed-my-life.

Nounopoulos, A., Ashby, J.S. and Gilman, R. (2006) 'Coping resources, per-fectionism, and academic performance among adolescents.' *Psychology in the Schools 43*, 5, 613–622.

Nugent, S. (2000) 'Perfectionism: Its manifestations and classroom-based interventions.' *Journal of Advanced Academics 11*, 4, 215–221.

Obholzer, A. and Roberts, V.Z. (1994) *The Unconscious at Work: Individual and Organizational Stress in the Human Services*. East Sussex: Routledge.

O'Connor, R.C., Rasmussen, S. and Hawton, K. (2010) 'Predicting depression, anxiety and self-harm in adolescents: The role of perfectionism and acute life stress.' *Behaviour Research and Therapy 48*, 1, 52–59.

Öngen, D.E. (2009) 'The relationships between perfectionism and aggression among adolescents.' *Procedia Social and Behavioral Sciences 1*, 1073–1077.

Onwuegbuzie, A.J. and Daley, C. (1999) 'Perfectionism and statistics anxiety.' *Personality and Individual Differences 26*, 1089–1102.

Owen, J. (2013) 'A third of children in Britain have had suicidal thoughts.' Accessed on 5 February 2015 at www.independent.co.uk/life-style/health-and-families/health-news/a-third-of-children-in-britain-have-had-suicidal-thoughts-8688940.html.

Padash, Z., Moradi, A. and Saadat, E. (2014) 'The effectiveness of psychotherapy training based on Frisch's theory on perfectionism.' *Interdisciplinary Journal of Contemporary Research in Business 5*, 10, 142–153.

Park, J., Storch, E., Pinto, A. and Lewin, A. (2015) 'Obsessive-compulsive personality traits in youth with obsessive-compulsive disorder.' *Child Psychiatry and Human Development, 47*, 22, 1–10.

Pembroke, N. (2012) 'Pastoral care for shame-based perfectionism.' *Pastoral Psychology 61*, 2, 245–258.

Pett, M. (2012) *The Girl Who Never Made Mistakes*. Naperville, IL: Sourcebooks.

Pleva, J. and Wade, T.D. (2007) 'Guided self-help versus pure self-help for perfectionism: A randomized controlled trial.' *Behaviour Research and Therapy 45*, 5, 849–861.

Precey, M. (2015) 'Teacher stress levels in England "soaring", data shows.' Accessed on 19 March 2015 at www.bbc.co.uk/news/education-31921457.

Prochaska, J. and DiClemente, C.C. (1983) *The Transtheoretical Approach: Towards a Systematic Eclectic Framework*. Homewood, IL: Dow Jones Irwin.

Psychcentral (2014) 'Kanye West: The only perfectionist.' Accessed on 5 November 2019 at www.blogs.psychcentral.com/celebrity/2014/07/kanye-west-the-only-perfectionist.

Ratcliffe, R. (2014) 'The verdict on Ofsted: "requires improvement"?' Accessed on 5 September 2015 at www.theguardian.com/education/2014/oct/28/-sp-verdict-ofsted-requires-improvement.

Rice, K.G., Ashby, J.S. and Gilman, R. (2011) 'Classifying adolescent perfectionists.' *Psychological Assessment 23*, 3, 563.

Rice, K.G., Leever, B.A., Noggle, C.A. and Lapsley, D.K. (2007) 'Perfectionism and depressive symptoms in early adolescence.' *Psychology in the Schools 44*, 2, 139–156.

Rice, K.G., Neimeyer, G.J. and Taylor, J.M. (2011) 'Efficacy of Coherence Therapy in the treatment of procrastination and perfectionism.' *Counseling Outcome Research and Evaluation 2*, 2, 126–136.

Rice, K.G. and Preusser, K.J. (2002) 'The adaptive/maladaptive perfectionism scale.' *Measurement and Evaluation in Counseling and Development 34*, 210–222.

Rimm, S. (2007) 'What's wrong with perfect? Clinical perspectives on perfectionism and underachievement.' *Gifted Education International 23*, 3, 246–253.

Rivière, J. and Douilliez, C. (2017) 'Perfectionism, rumination, and gender are related to symptoms of eating disorders: A moderated mediation model.' *Personality and Individual Differences 116*, 63–68.

Roedell, W.C. (1984) 'Vulnerabilities of highly gifted children.' *Roeper Review 6*, 3, 127–130.

Rotter, J. (1954) *Social Learning and Clinical Psychology.* Upper Saddle River, NJ: Prentice-Hall.

Roxborough, H.M., Hewitt, P.L., Kaldas, J., Flett, G.L., Caelian, C.M., Sherry, S. and Sherry, D.L. (2012) 'Perfectionistic self-presentation, social prescribed perfectionism, and suicide in youth: A test of the Perfectionism Social Discrimination Model.' *Suicide and Life-Threatening Behavior 42*, 217–233.

Royal College of Paediatrics and Child Health (2015). In D. Whitworth (ed.), 'Schools 'struggling to cope' with students self-harming.' Accessed on 20 February 2015 at www.bbc.co.uk/newsbeat/30695657.

Salzberger-Wittenberg, G., Williams, E. and Osborne, E. (1999) *Emotional Experience of Learning and Teaching.* London: Routledge, Taylor and Francis Group.

Samaritans (2015) 'Rise in suicides show the need to work together to tackle inequalities.' Accessed on 20 February 2015 at www.samaritans.org/news/rise-suicides-shows-need-work-together-tackle-inequalities.

Saviz, M. and Naeini, A.Z. (2014) 'The examination of the relationship between perfectionism and academic burnout as well as academic achievement of college students.' *Interdisciplinary Journal of Contemporary Research in Business 6*, 1, 148–164.

Schwartz, J.P., Grammas, D.L., Sutherland, R.J., Siffert, J. and Bush-King-I. (2010) 'Masculine gender roles and differentiation: Predictors of body image and self-objectification in men.' *Psychology of Men and Masculinity 11*, 3, 208–224.

Shafran, R., Cooper, Z. and Fairburn, C.G. (2002) 'Clinical perfectionism: A cognitive-behavioural analysis.' *Behaviour Research and Therapy 40*, 773–791.

Shafran, R., Egan, S. and Wade, T. (2010) Overcoming Perfectionism: A Self-Help Guide Using Cognitive-Behavioural Techniques. London: Robinson.

Shafran, R. and Mansell, W. (2001) 'Perfectionism and psychopathology: A review of research and treatment.' *Clinical Psychology Review 21*, 879–906.

Shaunessy, E. (2011) 'Mean levels and correlates of perfectionism in International Baccalaureate and general education students.' *High Ability Studies 22*, 1, 61–77.

Shih, S.S. (2012) 'An examination of academic burnout versus work engagement among Taiwanese adolescents.' *Journal of Educational Research 105*, 286–298.

Siegel, D. (2020) 'The Healthy Mind Platter.' Accessed on 1 April 2020 at https://www.drdansiegel.com/resources/healthy_mind_platter.

Siegle, D. and Schuler, P.A. (2000) 'Perfectionism differences in gifted middle school students.' *Roeper Review 23*, 1, 39–44.

Smith, M.M., Sherry, S.B., Chen, S., Saklofske, D.H., Mushquash, C., Flett, G.L. and Hewitt, P.L. (2017) 'The perniciousness of perfectionism: A meta-analytic review of the perfectionism–suicide relationship.' *Journal of Personality 86*, 3, 522–542.

Snaith, L. (2015) 'Blog: Early intervention and continued momentum.' Accessed on 20 February 2015 at www.rcpch.ac.uk/news/blog-early-intervention-and-continued-momentum.

Sorotzkin, B. (1998) 'Understanding and treating perfectionism in religious adolescents.' *Psychotherapy: Theory, Research, Practice, Training 35*, 87–95.

Sporting News (2014) '"Perfectionist" Williams her harshest critic.' Accessed on 5 November 2019 at www.sportingnews.com/au/other-sports/news/perfectionist-williams-her-harshest-critic/qm74i82ukfre1ce4jczwgm671.

Squires, G. (2001) 'Using cognitive behavioural psychology with groups of pupils to improve self-control of behaviour.' *Educational Psychology in Practice 17*, 4, 317–335.

Starley, D. (2018) 'Perfectionism: A challenging but worthwhile research area for educational psychology.' *Educational Psychology in Practice 35*, 2, 121–146.

Steele, A.L., Waite, S., Egan, S.J., Finnigan, J., Handley, A. and Wade, T.D. (2013) 'Psycho-education and group cognitive-behavioural therapy for clinical perfectionism: A case-series evaluation.' *Behavioural and Cognitive Psychotherapy 41*, 2, 129–143.

Stoeber, J. (1998) 'The Frost Multidimensional Perfectionism Scale revisited: More perfect with four (instead of six) dimensions.' *Personality and Individual Differences 24*, 481–491.

Stoeber, J. and Damian, L.E. (2014) 'The Clinical Perfectionism Questionnaire: Further evidence for two factors capturing perfectionistic strivings and concerns.' *Personality and Individual Differences 61–62*, 38–42

Stoeber, J. and Eysenck, M.W. (2008) 'Perfectionism and efficiency: Accuracy, response bias, and invested time in proof-reading performance.' *Journal of Research in Personality 42*, 6, 1673–1678.

Stoll, O., Lau, A. and Stoeber, J. (2008) 'Perfectionism and performance in a new basketball training task: Does striving for perfection enhance or undermine performance?' *Psychology of Sport and Exercise 9*, 5, 620–629.

Stornelli, D., Flett, G.L. and Hewitt, P.L. (2009) 'Perfectionism, achievement, and affect in children: A comparison of students from gifted, arts, and regular programs.' *Canadian Journal of School Psychology 24*, 4, 267–283.

Study.com (2019) 'Good careers for perfectionists.' Accessed on 5 November 2019 at www.study.com/articles/good_careers_for_perfectionists.html.

Szymanski, J. (2011) *The Perfectionist's Handbook.* Hoboken, NJ: John Wiley and Sons Inc.

Thorpe, E. and Nettelbeck. T. (2014) 'Testing if healthy perfectionism enhances academic achievement in Australian secondary school students.' *Journal of Educational and Developmental Psychology 4*, 2, 1–9.

Times, The (2015) 'Youth betrayed.' Accessed on 20 February 2015 at www.thetimes.co.uk/tto/opinion/leaders/article4359634.ece.

Törnblom, A.W., Werbart, A. and Rydelius, P.A. (2013) 'Shame behind the masks: The parents' perspective on their sons' suicide.' *Archives of Suicide Research 17*, 3, 242–261.

Tracy, J.L. and Robins, R.W. (2004) 'Putting the self into self-conscious emotions: A theoretical model.' *Psychological Inquiry 15*, 103–125.

Triggle, N. (2015) 'Child mental health faces "complex and severe" problems.' Accessed on 20 February 2015 at www.bbc.co.uk/news.health-31543213.

Udorie, J.E. (2015) 'Social media is harming the mental health of teenagers. The state has to act.' Accessed on 16 November 2015 at www.theguardian.com/commentisfree/2015/sep/16/social-media-mental-health-teenagers-government-pshe-lessons.

van Hanswijck de Jonge, L. and Waller, G. (2003) 'Perfectionism levels in African-American and Caucasian adolescents.' *Personality and Individual Differences 34*, 8, 1447–1451.

Wang, K.T., Yuen, M. and Slaney, R.B. (2009) 'Perfectionism, depression, loneliness, and life satisfaction: A study of high school students in Hong Kong.' *The Counseling Psychologist 37*, 249–274.

Weisinger, H. and Lobsenz, N.M. (1981) *Nobody's Perfect: How to Give Criticism and Get Results.* Los Angeles, CA: Stratford Press.

Whitney, J., Easter, A. and Tchanturia, K. (2008) 'Service users' feedback on cognitive training in the treatment of anorexia nervosa: A qualitative study.' *International Journal of Eating Disorder 41*, 6, 542–550.

Whitworth, D. (2015) 'Schools "struggling to cope" with students self-harming.' Accessed on 20 February 2015 at www.bbc.co.uk/newsbeat/30695657.

World Health Organisation (2019) 'Suicide.' Accessed on 5 November 2019 at www.who.int/en/news-room/fact-sheets/detail/suicide.

Winnicott, D. (1953) 'Transitional objects and transitional phenomena – a study of the first not-me possession.' *International Journal of Psycho-Analysis 34*, 88–97.

Yerkes, R.M. and Dodson, J.D. (1908) 'The relation of strength of stimulus to rapidity of habit-formation.' *Journal of Comparative Neurology and Psychology 18*, 5, 459–482.

Zhang, B. and Cai, T. (2012) 'Coping styles and self-esteem as mediators of the perfectionism-depression relationship among Chinese undergraduates.' *Social Behavior and Personality: An International Journal 40*, 157–168.

Zousel, M.L., Rule, A.C. and Logan, S.R. (2013) 'Teaching primary grade students perfectionism through cartoons compared to bibliotherapy.' *International Electronic Journal of Elementary Education 5*, 2, 199–218.

Further Reading

For those wishing to read more about the topic and related areas, I would recommend the following books:

- Brené Brown (2012) *Daring Greatly*. London: Penguin.

- Tal Ben-Shahar (2008) *Happier*. Berkshire: McGraw-Hill.

- Elizabeth Day (2019). *How to Fail*. London: 4th Estate.

- Jill L. Adelson & Hope E. Wilson (2009).*Letting Go of Perfect: Overcoming Perfectionism in Kids*. Waco, TX: Prufrock Press Inc.

- Carol Dweck (2006) *Mindset: The New Psychology of Success*. New York: Random House.

- Roz Shafran, Sarah Egan & Tracey Wade (2010) *Overcoming Perfectionism: A Self-Help Guide Using Cognitive-Behavioural Techniques*. London: Robinson.

- Pavel Somov (2010) *Present Perfect: A Mindfulness Approach*. Oakland, CA: New Harbinger Publications, Inc.

- Brené Brown (2010) *The Gifts of Imperfection*. Minnesota, MN: Hazelden.

- Tal Ben-Shahar (2009) *The Pursuit of Perfect*. Berkshire: McGraw-Hill.

- Thomas S. Greenspon (2007) *What to Do When Good Enough Isn't Good Enough*. Minneapolis, MN: Free Spirit Publishing Inc.

- Martin M. Antony & Richard P. Swinson (2008) *When Perfect Isn't Good Enough*. Oakland, CA: New Harbinger Publications, Inc.